We Were Cowboys

Copyright ©Eddie Baise 2017
ISBN-13: 978-1979498074
ISBN-10: 1979498075

This is a true story as I remember it, about just a few of the many adventures I shared with my best friend, beginning somewhere in the mid-1960's.

Dedicated
In
Memory
Of
My Best Friend
Robby Gowin
1956-1994

Special thanks to Carolyn Paul Branch.
Had it not been for her encouragement, help and
expertise, this book would not have been written.

We Were Cowboys

A Memoir
Eddie Baise

CONTENTS

I Wanna be a Cowboy..........................1

A Night Away From Hom....................4

Joint Sience Project...........................16

Panther on the Loose........................19

Penny Loafers..................................23

Boots at Last...................................26

Bill was Gone...................................29

My First Shoes.................................31

Big Red, an Outlaw..........................34

Revolvers and Racehorses..................38

I Landed a Job................................42

Shortess Cattle Drive Ever.................47

The Red Roan.................................52

Wild Cow Milkin..............................58

Motorcycle Ride...............................63

Kawasaki 900 Z1.............................67

Twenty Bucks the Hard Way..............72

Fall Round-up.................................76

Surprisingly Shocked..........................81
Lessons for an Un-Broke Colt.............84
Larry is Gone on Vacation...................87
Money Round...94
A Bucking Appaloosa...........................98
Chute Doggin......................................102
A Lost Calf..106
A Friday Night Fight.........................110
Robby Leaves Home..........................120
One Last Ride....................................123
The Beginning of the End..................127

I WANNA BE A COWBOY

Our family inherited a black and white pony one summer. Apparently, the pony's owners were moving out of state and there was no way to take the Shetland along. Dad patched the hog lot fence just well enough to keep Ole Bill corralled. It wasn't long before we realized Bill didn't care much about being caught, so Dad made a pony-sized collar with a long chain attached to slip around his neck. The chain wasn't heavy, but it was long enough in the event I got within a few feet of the un-cooperative beast, I could step on the chain and have a chance to hold him. Bill may have been a dumb animal, but he was smart enough to learn just how long the chain was. If I wasn't in tall grass and he could see the end of the chain, he wasn't going to be caught. Once I had a hand on the chain, he'd stop his illusive tendencies and let me handle him.

I had no prior knowledge of horse handling, so it was a long process for me to learn the fundamentals. I don't know if a saddle came with the pony, but at some point, one became available and I rode every chance I had or every chance I was able to catch Bill. Like most other ponies, Bill rarely missed an opportunity to step on my toes, spook at nothing, refuse to move when asked, or run under a low hanging limb or bush to brush me off when riding.

I loved my new-found friend and made an effort to gain more knowledge and skills to become a better horseman. Being inspired by watching movies of John Wayne, Bonanza and other western shows on my grandma's blurry television, I just knew what I wanted to be when I grew up. I wanted to be a cowboy.

I told my mom one evening we needed to go to Zim's, the local men and boys store in Fulton this coming Saturday so Dad could buy me some cowboy boots.

"You don't need any cowboy boots."

"But I need them to be a cowboy. I wanna be a cowboy."

"I don't care. As long as I'm your mother, you aren't getting any boots, especially cowboy boots!"

"How can I be a real cowboy without cowboy boots?"

"I don't care. You're not getting any."

We Were Cowboys

That was the end of that conversation. I wasn't at all happy about what Mom had said, but I knew there was no reason to pursue the issue. I was stuck with the most economical foot ware my folks could afford at the time, the usual brown, low-heeled, medium-top, lace-up boots, with the three hooks and cotton laces.

Eddie Baise

A NIGHT AWAY FROM HOME

The bus hadn't even begun to slow down and we were out of our seats, headed to the front. Robby was in the lead, I was next, then Rusty and Nita, Robby's older siblings. As the driver applied the brakes, we had to lean back just to keep from being thrown forward as the bus lost momentum. When the doors opened, Robby jumped from the top step and hit the gravel drive at a run. Only a few steps behind, I tried catching up as we raced the one-hundred-fifty yards to the house.

Robby had invited me to stay overnight at his house, something we had discussed on several occasions. I had never stayed overnight at anyone else's home unless it was my grandparents in Mexico or my grandmothers' home in Fulton. I was excited and apprehensive at the same time.

Robby and I had been acquainted through church and we both belonged to the same 4-H club. Up to this point, Sundays, or at the monthly club meetings was the only time we saw each other. We previously attended separate one-room schools, Robby at Pew and I went to Sheets. However, due to redistricting and consolidating all the little schools into larger centrally located and more modern facilities, we both went to the school in Calwood. In the short period of time that we had been together, we shared our interests with horses and had become best friends.

I was two steps behind Robby when he hit the porch and opened the door. He ran into the living room stopping just long enough to pull off his ruff-out cowboy boots.

"Take off your shoes. Mom doesn't like us to walk on the carpet with our boots on. Hi Mom, Eddie's here!"

Edith greeted me as I unlaced my shoes and she told Robby to get out of his school clothes. In a matter of what seemed seconds, he had stripped down to his white cotton briefs and donned a pair of blue jean cutoffs. I hadn't brought old clothes to change into, only a clean change for the following day, so I didn't undress.

"Come on, we have to go down to the barn and doctor a colt down there." he said, "Then, we can play."

Just about as fast as we had entered the house, we exited only slowing down enough for me to slip on my shoes and get them laced just enough to keep them from falling off. Then, we hurriedly headed towards the old barn behind the house. The low evening sun made the dust clouds Robby was kicking up with his bare feet sparkle. Careful to not step in the fresh piles of green manure left by the loose horses in the pasture, we either jumped over them or went just off of the dry trail to get around them. Stopping at an old shed, Robby opened the door, stepped in and retrieved a can and wooden paddle. The distinct aroma of smoke escaped the opening of the once used smokehouse, now used solely for storage. I questioned Robby about the items in his hands.

"What's that?"

"It's pine-tar. There's a colt in the barn with distemper. We dip the paddle in the bucket of pine-tar and dob it in the colts' throat a couple times. Dad says it will cure the distemper."

Pulling the metal lid off the gallon sized can revealed an extra thick, black liquid with an indescribable smell. It was sort of sweet, yet very strong. Dipping deep into the pail with the crude homemade spatula, Robby told me to open the ill colts' mouth so he could do the doctoring as prescribed. The patient made a gagging sound each time Robby poked the paddle down its mouth. That made it apparent the colt didn't like taking medicine any better than I did. After repeated applications, we were able to get enough of the nasty syrup down the horse (and on us) to satisfy Robby. We went back to the smokehouse, placed the can and paddle on the wooden floor and we were off to the house at a fast pace. We had playing to do.

We were just messing around in the yard, talking and looking at more of the horses he and his family had. We stopped at a small pasture in front of the house, which had three horses in it. Standing next to the board fence that divided yard from pasture with our arms resting on the middle rail, Robby started telling a little history of each animal grazing on the fescue grass.

"These are registered quarter horse mares," he explained. "Dad bought these and said we could start raising registered horses. They bring more money 'cause they are better than the stuff we've been riding."

I hadn't a clue about quarter horses, registered, more money. It didn't mean anything to me, but I agreed as if I knew just what he was telling me.

Bored at being still way too long, Robby climbed up onto the top rail of the three board fence and began walking down its length as if it was a tightrope. Swaying back and forth, he eventually lost his balance just a short distance from me. Robby fell downward, raking his side as he fell. Lying in a heap, he grasped his side and began to squirm as if he was hurt badly. He rolled around with a grimaced face and his hands covering his wounds. I didn't know how bad he was hurt and all I could do was watch.

At about the same time as Robby hit the hard, dry dirt, his dad pulled in the drive. Apparently, he wasn't supposed to be on the fence, or he didn't want his dad knowing he had gotten hurt because when he heard the truck coming down the drive, he was up moving around the yard as if nothing had happened. Wiping the moisture from his still grimacing face, "Come on, we need to go in."

Moving towards the back of the house to avoid his dad, we made a half circle around the back of the house and into the walk-out basement. We hung out there in the dimly lit and musty smelling basement for a short time until Edith called us for supper.

Slowly climbing the wooden staircase from the lower level up to the living room, Robby was still trying to avoid a confrontation with his dad. Edith told us to get cleaned up and made a point to remind us to get the remnants of the pine tar off as well.

"I don't want to smell that awful stuff while we're eating."

I didn't know where Bob had disappeared to, but so far, Robby was in the clear.

Rusty had made it to the bathroom first and had just finished wiping his hands dry when the pair of us turned the corner into the small room. I was already in awe because they had hot running water. I thought to myself how lucky Robby and his family was, having all the nice things that my family didn't, carpet on the floor, running water and a full-size bathtub that had running hot water as well. Man, I thought they must be really rich!

Scuffling at the sink, Robby and I splashed water out of the sink and onto the floor. The towel that was hanging in the bathroom was the closest thing we could find to mop up the wet floor. Hanging the heavily soaked towel back on the rack, we headed back down the hall pausing briefly for Robby to find a t-shirt to cover his battle scars.

We went into the kitchen where the smell of something good was cooking.

"Eddie, you like noodles?" Edith asked.

"Heck yes."

"Good. Robby, you can set the plates please."

Grabbing a big stack of mismatched plates off the counter, Robby made a complete circle around the big yellow table dispensing a plate every so often. By the time the table was set, Bob had made his entrance and set down at the end of the table.

I had never met Robby's Dad before, only his mother. He was shorter than Edith by some bit, white hair, where there was hair and worn bibs. I noticed his hands were very rugged and had some fingers missing from one hand. He seemed quiet but polite.

"Hello," he said as he looked at my skinny body sitting right next to him.

Edith started placing bowls of food on the metal table and by the time she had finished, there was hardly a space left. The only time I had seen this much food at one time on a single table was at Thanksgiving or Christmas. When Rusty and Nita finally sat down at the table, Edith was also getting to her chair. Bowls heaping full of meat and vegetables began to go past my nose and I dipped a little bit out of each one until the noodles reached my place at the table. I had to stop for a moment to make sure they were in fact noodles. They weren't noodles like I'd ever seen before. My mother had made noodles many times, but never noodles like these. These weren't the pour-out-of-the-bag–store-bought variety, these were homemade. Each one was nearly a foot long, thick, wide and juicy. They tasted even better than they looked. I could have made a meal out of just noodles.

As we ate, there were small conversations of varied topics, mostly about school. The bowls made their way around the table again and again until most of the contents were completely dispatched. Bob was buttering a piece of white bread and finally looked at Robby asking about his side.

"Raise that shirt and let me see what you did."

Pulling on the white t-shirt that clung to the sweat created by the kitchen heat, Robby revealed a big red, strawberry shaped, abrasion that oozed tiny bits of blood, especially at each rib, which had taken the brunt of the fall.

"I guess by God you'll not do that again," in a low, very unsympathetic tone. He topped the buttered slice of bread with a hot homemade rhubarb desert Edith had made, "You boys get the dishes cleaned up." I knew without being told, that meant me as well.

Rusty began scraping the un-eaten scraps onto one plate to give to the hounds, while Robby and I washed and dried. Edith remained in the kitchen to help with the dishes and tidy up. There seemed to be no end to the colossal pile and it took a while to get the task completed. The Gowin family was big in comparison to mine and they consumed lots of food and had lots of dishes to clean.

Sunshine was all gone by the time we had finished washing the dishes and we were told to go get a bath.

Robby told me, "Come on, we can do it at the same time," and we hastily walked to the bathroom. Robby turned the hot water tap on and in seconds there was steaming hot water flowing into the huge cast-iron tub. Testing the warmth with his hand, he turned the cold on to make the temperature just right.

As the water neared the top rim of the tub, we removed our clothes and threw them in a heap on the floor. When the both of us climbed into the warm bath water, it was to the point of overflowing and any movement made water slosh out onto the floor.

We had been in the tub for some time when Edith poked her head in the door, embarrassing me, and told us to get out and wipe up the spilled water. We got out, cleaned up the bathroom and Robby went to his and Rusty's room.

In my haste, I hadn't got any clean clothes to dress with after the bath. Looking around the corner, I could see Edith sitting in a big chair in the living room straight down the hall. I was very modest and I didn't want her to see my naked body again, so I picked my dirty t-shirt off the wet floor, covered my private parts and quickly darted the short distance into the privacy of Robby's room.

Robby slipped on underwear and I pulled on a pair of blue jeans over my briefs to retire to the living room where everyone else was watching television. We laid on the warm carpet covered floor, chins on the palms of our hands and eyes gazing at the screen until it was bedtime.

The evening had been very exciting for me. I was still overloaded from supper and even though it was crowded with both Robby and me in the small twin-sized bed, sleep came rather quickly. Edith only had to tell us twice, "Get to sleep!"

Awakened by the bright light being flipped on and "Time to get up," I could smell the aroma of bacon being fried. I made a trip to the bathroom and when I returned to the bedroom to get dressed, I found Robby had pulled the covers over his head trying to sleep just a bit longer. I was sitting on the edge of the bed fully dressed, waiting for him to get up and his mother returned once more,

"I'm not telling you again. Get up. How many pancakes do you want Eddie"?

"Two," I replied.

"Just two?"

"Yes, thank you."

Blinking from the light, Robby moved the covers down and slowly dug around the four-drawered dresser looking for pants to put on. He pulled a short sleeve shirt from the closet and buttoned it as we walked to the kitchen.

Once more, Edith had prepared a meal that looked as if she could have fed half the neighbors as well as her own family. I saw two plates sitting on the table, one piled high with bacon and the other with fried eggs. I sat down in the same spot I had the night before and a plate with two plate size pancakes was placed in front of me.

"Get some eggs and bacon."

My brothers and I were taught if we put it on our plate, we had to eat it all. I wasn't sure if I could eat all the pancakes I had received, but I had asked for two and I would bust if I had to in order to get them consumed.

I placed two pieces of bacon and one egg alongside the huge, syrup covered pancakes and dug in. By the time I'd finished, I felt as though I couldn't take a step. I was full to say the least.

"The bus will be here soon. You boys better get to moving." Edith began the task of cleaning up after the morning meal.

None of the four of us wanted to go to school very badly. We slowly walked up the gravel lane, reaching the blacktopped road just in time to see the bus coming into view around the corner. After one additional stop, the yellow bus stopped at our location and the doors swung open. The four of us climbed up the steps of the noisy, kid crowded vehicle, sat down and rode the short distance to school.

As slow as molasses pouring from a can, my day at school went as equally slow. Our teacher mundanely lecturing one class and then, another. On one hand I could hardly wait for the day to be over and the other, I knew I had to go back to my own home that did not provide all the nice things I'd been indulging in for the last twenty-four hours.

As the bus turned into the drive at my house, I thanked my friend for the last evening and asked if maybe we could do it once more in the future.

"Of course", he assured me and I walked down the steps preparing to re-enter the dull world I felt I existed in. I watched the bus turn around,

We Were Cowboys

waved so long to my buddy and began to think about the chores that awaited me.

Eddie Baise

JOINT SCIENCE PROJECT

Our teacher, Mrs. Benskin, told the class we were to do a report for a science project. It didn't have to be anything too complicated but did need to relate to some scientific theory. I wasn't able to think of any subject that suited me until my best friend approached me about going together on a project. He explained his theory to me and I thought it was a pretty good idea. We went to the teacher to find out if she would allow us to work on this project together. She obviously wanted to know what we had in mind. We didn't want to give our project secret out completely, but after some explanation, she gave us the okay.

Robby and I began researching and getting our supplies gathered up, a little each night. My dad was good at saving stuff, so we mostly dug around my place and found everything we needed. That is, everything except 2 D size batteries. I told Robby we could "borrow" the ones out of my dad's flashlight, but we had to make sure we put them back each time we used them.

We Were Cowboys

We spent a week or so, getting everything in order, cutting a couple blocks of wood, shaping a piece of sheet metal to the proper size and shape and wrapping copper wire around several 16 penny nails. When we weren't working on the project, we were studying or riding our horses.

One evening we proudly put all the components together hoping everything was right. I snuck into the kitchen where Dad kept the flashlight and grabbed the batteries from it. With some minor adjusting we were able to fit the batteries in the right place. We looked at each other as if to say, "you do it, no you do it".

I pushed the button and nothing. Then it was that "now what" look. We took turns looking at our assembly and adjusting our crude configuration of parts. One more push of the button and alas, it clicked. Hot Dang, we had her going.

The morning we were to give our report, Robby and I each loaded up our half of the project to haul to school. I almost forgot the batteries in my haste but did manage to get them loaded as well.

Mrs. Benskin told us it was time to reveal our secret and give our project report. Robby began setting up his portion and I set mine up as well. I handed him one of the batteries and took one for myself. As we were setting up, Mrs. Benskin was looking over our shoulder to see just what we had. I looked her way and she was smiling a bit, so I thought maybe this might work out okay.

"Tell the class what you have," she said.

Although Robby was never short on words, he wasn't going to do any public speaking if he could get out of it, but he punched the button several times to click out dot, dot, dot, dash, dash, dash, dot, dot, dot.

"That was "S O S in Morse code," I told the class.

We had spent our time learning the Morse code and building a pair of working telegraphs. We clicked out a couple more "messages" and concluded our report.

There were some remains of old telephone lines on cedar poles along the blacktop that ran in front of Robby's house. We were only ten or eleven, but had big ideas. He and I discussed trying to use those lines to send messages to each other. Of course, other adventures lay ahead of us and the long-distance telegraph project fell to the side and was forgotten.

I don't think my dad ever figured out why those batteries were dead the next time he needed a flashlight.

We Were Cowboys

PANTHER ON THE LOOSE

A few weeks after my initial stay with Robby and his family, he invited me over once again. I spent my usual twenty minutes one afternoon after school catching Bill, so I could ride to his house for supper. We had made plans for me to ride over, ride around after supper, then spend the night. The next morning we would go to school and then I would ride back home the next evening after school.

After getting my trusty long-haired steed brushed and saddled, I mounted up for the three-mile ride. I headed through the woods and came out on the road on the other side of Lake Calwood. Continuing up the road at a snail's pace, we headed for our final destination now just two and a half miles away. I managed to get ole Bill as far as Mosts' corner and the Fairview Cemetery. That's when he when he decided he was not about to go any further away from home. As an amateur horseman, I did everything I could think of to get that little paint pony to go in the direction of Robby's house.

Mrs. Most surely must have seen me having trouble because she came out on the porch and made a panicked comment about a black panther running loose in that area. Mrs. Most wasn't crazy, although many said she was and I doubted there was a panther anywhere near there. However, she was convinced there was and said that old pony had smelled it to the point of being too scared to go on. At best, all Mrs. Most's verbal imagination had achieved was saturating my young mind with notions of some wild black beast ripping my prized pony to pieces.

Reaching slightly above my head, I pulled a limb of persuasion from a peach tree in her yard and was able to motivate Bill in the proper direction. By the time I had made it to Robby's, it was getting close to dark. My trip had taken me nearly three hours to complete.

Once my long and eventful trip had ended, I went right to the barn and Robby hurriedly helped un-saddle my pony. We ran into the house that loomed the aroma of a delicious home cooked meal and I was told to clean up. Robby's mother voiced her concern about my lengthy trip, so I explained about the pony's reluctance to go too far from home, Mrs. Most and the panther she said was on the loose in the woods.

We Were Cowboys

"There's no panther on the loose," as she set a plate on the table for me.

The family had already eaten by the time I arrived, but she had kept a plate warm for me and I ate my late supper with several heaping helpings of ribbing to go along with it. Our carefully laid plan had not gone as well as we thought it should have and bedtime arrived before there was time to do much else.

Getting up to a hot home-cooked breakfast was something I rarely enjoyed at my home, so I was sitting at the table the next morning in anticipation of bacon and eggs. Instead, Robby's mom had chosen to make biscuits and sausage gravy. I was not disappointed with her choice. I simply couldn't imagine eating like this every day.

As usual, for me, school was as boring as ever. It wasn't that I disliked school, or I didn't think I really needed to be there, I didn't care for the teacher mostly. She had her favorite students, the smart ones, and I did not fit the mold and Robby even less. I think those issues only helped tighten the bond between Robby and me.

Eventually, classes did let out and we were back at Robby's. I was dreading the trip home on my cantankerous spotted pony but knew that I had to do it. Robby took his stuff inside without me and came back out with a huge smile on his face.

"Mom told me to saddle up and ride to your house with you, so maybe that way you'd get there better."

Together we went to the barn, saddled both our mounts and began my homeward trek.

Without a doubt, Mrs. Most had nothing better to do except look out her windows in search of some imaginary threat to anyone that happened past her place. Just as before, she exited her house to caution Robby and me about the big black panther that lurked the nearby woods just waiting for an unsuspecting meal to come within reach of those long claws and nasty white teeth. We made the corner by the cemetery and laughed as we continued towards the lake just ahead.

Like a lot of kids, we laughed, made un-kind jokes about Mrs. Most and played as much as we rode. The cross-country ride was over way sooner than either of us wanted.

After un-saddling, Bill seemed happy to be home in his own little hog lot pasture, even though wearing his long chain was a necessity. With a nod, I watched Robby turn his horse to the west and ride off, disappearing just over the hill a quarter mile away.

PENNY LOAFERS

I had repeatedly asked my mother for cowboy boots. I always got the same answer from her, "NO!"

If I asked why not, it was "Just because."

Since I wasn't buying the shoes at that time, my brothers and I got to wear brown, lace-up work boots and we had to make them last as long as possible. I had worn mine until the sole had come loose and was flapping with each step I took.

My brothers and I had gone to my grandmothers in Fulton one afternoon and she noticed my loose shoe sole. She told me there was a pair of shoes she had saved upstairs in a box and I was to go get them. She went on to explain, one of my cousins had out-grown them and they were too good to throw away. I went to the designated box where I found the saved shoes, an old dried out pair of black penny loafers. I told Grandma I really didn't want the loafers because they were too big.

"I have to scoot my feet to keep them on. I can get along with the shoes I have for a while longer".

Eddie Baise

She insisted they were better than the worn-out shoes I was wearing and I would grow into the black loafers. When Dad came in from work that evening, he thought it was a good idea to wear the slip-on shoes till he and Mom could get me a new pair of work shoes.

One Saturday night, I rode along with the Gowin family to the Rough Riders Saddle Club horse show. Once a month during the warm months, this saddle club put on a gathering for the adults and younger cowboys and cowgirls to show off their horsemanship.

Robby entered the pick-up race and wanted me to be his partner for the event. This was a timed event where one person was horseback, rode to the opposite end of the arena, picked up a person and the pair raced back to where the race started.

In order for us to be good at this, it was suggested we practice a few times in the field before entering the arena. We made several practice runs at it and figured we had this in the bag. There were a few pairs performing before our run, so we watched and discussed what we should do differently from their run in order to win the event. Then it was our turn to run.

I walked to the other end of the arena where Robby was to ride down, pick me up, turn and run back as fast as possible. I had been dumping dirt and grass out of Grandma's hand-me-down slippers all night and walking down through the tilled arena was no different. When I made it to the end of the arena, my shoes were half full of dirt and only the Lord knows what else.

    I turned and waited for the race to start. Within a matter of seconds, Robby was on his way to pick me up. Closer, closer, he's here, I reached for the horn and Robby had my arm pulling me on. The horse made the turn and we headed to the other end of the arena in a cloud of dust.

    After crossing the finish line, I slid down off the horses' hind end and hit the dirt in my socks. All I could hear was the spectators laughing. When I grabbed the saddle horn, the horse turned so hard there was enough force for the second-hand penny loafers to fly off across the arena. On a dead run, I headed to the other end of the arena in my sock feet to retrieve my shoes. The crowd was laughing and cheering the whole time.

    After collecting my lost footware, I headed to the truck to hide, but there was no hiding. Everyone had seen my performance and had gotten a good laugh out of it at my expense. I didn't let it bother me long though, Rusty was up next for musical tires with his white pony named Midnight and I wanted to watch them make their run.

Eddie Baise

BOOTS AT LAST

It had been a long and bitter fight, but now Mom and Dad were divorced. Dad kept the home place, my brother and I stayed with him and Mom moved to Millersburg.

Enduring their battle was very strenuous on me and I felt at times the only friend I had was my Shetland pony. It didn't matter how I was feeling, he was always there to console me. I bet I'd asked him a hundred times what had gone wrong or what had happened to cause this terrible event in my life. There was never an answer, but he was there to hug or to groom.

I struggled with life in general, but Bill was a constant source of relief for those days when it seemed all was lost. In time I healed, ever so slowly, but things got better.

Living with just my dad was very different than before. We didn't do much of anything but live from day to day. Dad went to work and my brother and I went to school. He did all he knew to do to make things okay for us, but times were more

We Were Cowboys

difficult than before. Money was tight and some of the things that once were commonplace, weren't any longer. Dad wasn't much of a cook, but we did not go hungry or miss any meals if we were home. Our clothes had to last as long as possible and sometimes a little longer than we really wanted them to.

My shoes had become quite worn. The laces had broken multiple times and I had skipped several holes just to get them tied with short, knotted laces. All the brown polish had disappeared quite some time ago and the heels had worn away exposing the nails that kept them in place. It was apparent I needed new shoes soon.

Saturday morning was the time we went to town to buy groceries or other supplies that were needed at home. After purchasing all the supplies we needed, I assumed we would be headed home right away. However, Dad turned off Market Street onto one of the side streets and parked in front of Zim's Men and Boys.

At the time I didn't put much thought into it, but that was where most of our clothes and shoes came from. Dad looked at me and said we were going in to buy me some new shoes. The thought of getting new shoes was always very exciting.

Going inside the store was a treat alone. The smell of polished leather boots and shoes on display was everywhere. Mr. Zimmerman greeted us as we entered and politely asked what he could do for us.

Dad motioned towards me and told him I needed shoes.

As expected, Mr. Zimmerman brought out a pair of the brown lace-up boots like I had been bought for years. I looked up at Dad and shyly asked if I could have boots instead of shoes this time. Much to my surprise, he said I could look at them.

I jumped up and started looking at all the choices available. There must have been twenty-five pair on display. Most however, were much too expensive and Dad said "no" until I saw a pair of Wellingtons.

They had a flat, low heel, but pulled on like boots in place of tied with laces. They weren't real cowboy boots, but close enough and they were also about the same price as the shoes I was used to wearing. Dad finally agreed to let me have the Wellington boots and Mr. Zimmerman left to locate a pair in my size.

After trying on a couple pair he'd brought out, I finally had a pair on that fit just right. He asked if I wanted them in the box or if I was going to wear them out the door. At long last, I was wearing a pair of boots and I wasn't about to take them off.

"I'm wearing them!"

BILL WAS GONE

Gene, one of the neighborhood boys, asked one day if I wanted to sell my old pony Bill. I explained he had been left with us years ago and the people that left him had intended on picking him up someday, but I also told him I would talk to my Dad about it.

Dad decided it had been years since we had heard from the actual owners and felt they weren't going to come back for him. He told me I could do whatever I wanted to with Bill.

I had outgrown Bill and had already bought a bigger horse, so I told the prospective buyer I would take twenty-five dollars for the pony. He agreed and said he'd come back and get him the following Saturday, that would give him time to fix fence enough to keep the pony from running off.

Saturday came and so did the neighbor. We went out to the lot to catch Bill and not surprisingly, Bill decided he didn't want to be caught.

The lot Bill was in wasn't very big, an acre at most, and was cross fenced. Gene and I devised a plan to corner Bill in the lot, get hold of the collar and chain that Dad kept on him and then slip a bridle in his mouth. We got close several times, but Bill would elude us time and time again.

We finally got him in a corner and began closing in on him. We got right up to the chain and Bill took off like a rocket, headed for the other side of the lot. In his excitement, Bill must have forgotten about that cross fence because he never slowed down a bit. He hit that fence with a full head of steam. When Bill's feet got tangled in the wire, it flipped him head over heels, landing on his back with a crash. It knocked the wind out of him just long enough for us to catch him at that point. Bill got to his feet and shook his head, panting like a racehorse.

I had pre-warned Gene about catching Bill and after this go-round I asked if he still wanted him. He did, and off they went, Gene proud as could be of his new ride.

I asked Gene several days later if he was able to catch that pony after turning him loose. He said only if he had a bucket of corn and tricked him into the barn where he could shut the door on him.

Gene kept the pony for a while, but got tired of those old pony antics and finally sold him.

We Were Cowboys

MY FIRST SHOES

I was about eleven when I purchased first horse from the local horsetrader. I'd had a pony before that, but this was a real full-size horse. He was a two-year-old sorrel Appaloosa gelding, fourteen hands high and green broke. I was so excited about my new horse, I gave my Grandpa Tate a call to tell him all about it. He had grown up working horses and I thought he would like to see what I had. He said it would be a few days before he could come over, but Grandpa showed up early the next morning all primed to take a look at that fine "steed" I'd acquired.

We got him out and Grandpa was telling me all the things that were right or wrong about him. I think it was about fifty good traits to fifty bad, but Grandpa finally gave me the "ok". He felt the horse would work out for me.

Grandpa was always good for a laugh. He asked me what I was going to call this sorrel gelding. I hadn't thought much about it and told him so.

"Well good," He said. "You probably shouldn't stick any kind of name to him."

I was kind of confused and he knew it, so I ask why not to name him. With a most serious face he said, "Well, you shouldn't name anything you might have to eat if times get hard".

I guess I must have just stood there dumbfounded for at least a couple seconds. He couldn't hold it in long and laughed at me.

Grandpa picked up one of the horses' front feet and inspected it for any problems. He then told me that because I had a horse, I was going to have to keep him shod.

"Shod? What's that?"

He explained I would have to put horseshoes on the horses' feet if I was going to do any amount of riding. I didn't know how to do that, but he said he would be willing to show me how.

He told me to go get a pencil and a piece of paper or cardboard. I did, and he placed the horses' front foot on the paper and traced around it. He explained he had done that so he could get shoes the right size and the next weekend he would come back so we could shoe the little horse.

Just as he had promised, Grandpa showed up and had four brand new steel horseshoes and a handful of nails. He got in the back of his car and pulled out a box of tools and a stand. He explained I needed the equipment to put those shoes on.

We Were Cowboys

All along I had it in my head Grandpa was going to do the shoeing and I was going to do the watching so I could catch on. That was not the case.

"You can't learn from watching. You're going to do it first hand, then you will know what to do".

Grandpa went on to explain what each tool was, it's intended purpose and showed me why the nails were shaped as they were.

That had to be the most tolerant two-year-old horse in Callaway County because I wrestled the poor beast around for two or two and a half hours to get those shiny metal shoes nailed on. It was the worst looking mess you could imagine, but Grandpa led me to believe it was first rate.

I'm not sure which one of us was the most tired, but between the three of us, the appy was shod.

After I got old enough to drive and improved my shoeing skills, from time to time Grandpa would have me come over to put shoes on some little horse or pony he had traded for. Every time he traded for some new animal, I would ask him "What'd you name him"?

We would laugh and reminisce about some critter one of us had, or the time when I was setting my first shoes on that poor little Appaloosa.

Eddie Baise

BIG RED: AN OUTLAW

On a Friday night, I rode down to the Montgomery horse auction with Bob and Robby. I had been without a horse for a couple months and spring was coming up so, I thought I might find something suitable to ride for the summer.

The three of us looked the stock over and made comments about several. Bob pointed out a couple he thought might work out for me, Robby liked a little bay filly and I picked a couple I thought I might keep my eye on. They always sold tack first, so we had plenty time to grab a snack in the kitchen and then hang out in the pens looking for that late horse that might come in.

About thirty minutes into the sale, the filly Robby liked came in the ring. She was a nice three-year-old, just started. I was nervous about bidding on a horse, so Bob said he would help me out. I didn't need any help with this horse because she started for way more than the one-hundred-fifty dollars I had in my pocket. So was the way of the auction for the biggest part of the night. Leaving the auction early was unheard of, so we were going to stay till the last horse ran through.

They had run seventy or eighty head through and this big red gelding was next. Bob had pointed this one out while we were in the back, but we hadn't really looked him over a lot. This three-year-old walked into the ring like he had done it a hundred times, nice and calm, even though he was green broke. The auctioneer started him out at fifty dollars and worked him up to ninety very quickly. I bid ninety-five and someone else bid a hundred. I bid once more and I had a nice gelding for a hundred and ten dollars.

Bob hadn't brought the trailer down, so we made arrangements for one of the neighbors to take the horse to his house. The next morning, we would swing by and pick up my horse at their place.

It was late when we left the auction and morning seemed to arrive quickly. We got over to the neighbors about ten. There in the corral was the gelding, but it wasn't the same horse I had bought the night before. It was the same horse, but he sure didn't act the same. It was a good thing he was in a small pen, or I don't know if we would have caught him.

Bob hauled the horse down to my place and we discussed the animal for a while. Finally, I decided to keep him penned up so I could get a hold of him when I wanted. Bob left and I ran in and called Grandpa Tate. I wanted to let him know I was the proud owner of more horseflesh. He said he was coming over to take a look.

Grandpa showed up and we headed down to the shed to look the gelding over. I got the door open and pulled the sorrel out into the sunlight. Grandpa stood there for a second or two and told me to get rid of the horse right away. Well, I didn't know what to think, so I asked him what was going on.

"Boy, you need to get rid of that outlaw right now. That son-of-a-bitch is no good for nothing but getting you hurt. Just look at his eyes and you can tell. That horse is nothing but trouble. I'm tellin ya' boy, you need to get rid of him." Then he got into his car and drove away.

I didn't know what to do, but I knew he wasn't right about this one.

I rode the red horse for a couple weeks and it became clear, maybe Grandpa wasn't wrong after all.

Climbing on Red was like riding a time bomb ready to blow the next second. After getting struck twice, once in the back and then once on the arm, I could see we were not going to get along.

Robby rode over one afternoon to see how I was getting along with the red devil. I told him I thought I was going to haul him to the next sell and let someone else have a go at him. Robby offered me my money back, stating he thought he could break him. I agreed to his offer and we saddled

We Were Cowboys

Red. I rode his horse and he rode Big Red to his new home.

Robby was a very determined wrangler. He had more experience and was better at handling horses than I was. I knew between the two of us, he would have a better chance of training Red than I would.

He did finally get a good handle on the big red horse and rode him for several years. However, the horse was always the same unpredictable animal as when I had purchased him. He hurt several people and Robby finally decided he needed a better, more trustworthy horse, so he sold him.

I guess Grandpa knew his horses after all.

Eddie Baise

REVOLVERS AND RACEHORSES

When I was about fourteen, I acquired a cap and ball revolver. It was a working replica of an 1851 Navy Colt and shot a 36-caliber ball using a dose of black powder. With summer replacing spring and school getting out, I spent a great deal of time on the banks of the Auxvasse Creek shooting cans and sticks that floated down with the flow of the water. Quite often, there would be an unsuspecting snake slithering quietly across the murky waters and I'd send a lead ball his way. As often as not, I'd score a hit. It didn't matter either way, with every shot there was a huge cloud of white smoke billowing out of the barrel from the stinky, burning powder and the violent splash of water would leave a muddy spot in the shallow water. It was something to do and kept me out of the house and out of trouble.

My Grandpa Tate was always one for trading and when he saw that revolver, he had to have it.

We Were Cowboys

He offered to trade a two-year-old brown mare for that cheap replica pistol.

I'd shot nearly twenty-five pounds of lead through the revolver and the frame was sprung so bad from shooting too heavy a load, Dad had to build the hammer up so it would strike the cap.

We discussed the matter and finally I was satisfied. I thought I would come out pretty fair on the deal, but only after getting him to agree to deliver the mare.

"Hell, I'll ride the mare here if I have to." He said.

I traded sight unseen.

When trading with Grandpa there was always a lesson to learn. The day he delivered the mare, I knew I had a lot more to learn about trading. My two-year-old mare I'd traded for sight unseen was probably closer to twenty than two. She was so old her bottom lip hung open –ALL THE TIME!!! She was poor and her backbone nearly drug the ground. She was swaybacked for sure.

I penned the mare up and started putting the grain to her. After a couple months on full grain, she began to gain a bit of weight and look a little better. I would ride nearly every day, but not too hard, just enough to kept her in shape.

One afternoon, Robby and I took off on a ride through what we knew as the Anders place. It was five hundred acres of the most beautiful piece of earth on the Auxvasse Creek. We'd made a fairly big circle and decided to head back to the house. Like most of the time, we were getting bored with the slow pace we had been riding at, so we kicked our mounts into a nice slow canter. The competitive urge swelled up in our young egos, the pace quickened and then the race was on.

My brown mare surprised me and was out in front pulling away from the young horse Robby was riding. Out across the field and through the tall grass, our horses were running as hard as we could make them go, their hooves beating out a rhythm as they struck the hard dry ground in nearly perfect unison.

Without warning, I was scooting head first through the fescue jungle, my mount somewhere behind me. When all the tumbling stopped, I stood to see just the head and ears of the brown mare sticking up in the tall grass. Robby was off to the side of me trying to stay mounted as his horse bucked like a rodeo bronc.

Robby got his horse under control and was laughing so hard he could barely sit in the saddle. I couldn't imagine what had happened as I went to gather the nearly invisibly mare. As I neared, I discovered her quietly standing in a washout that lay hidden in the tall, un-mowed hay. I was far enough ahead of Robby that he saw my mare fall head first in the deep ditch. He was able to get his young mount to jump over the crevice, which set it off to bucking after the jump. We laughed for a good ten minutes before I slipped over the edge of the cracked sod and remounted my fallen racehorse.

That mare may have been old, but she had a good spirit. Grandpa didn't know he had traded off a derby winner and never figured out I'd gotten the better end of that deal, at least in my mind.

I was rarely satisfied with the horse of the time, but I kept the ole brown mare for a couple summers and then traded her for a younger, one-eyed gelding.

Eddie Baise

I LANDED A JOB

I had a part-time weekend job working at a filling station in Kingdom City but it only paid just enough to keep gas in my car. My best friend Robby had landed a full-time job at a development company mowing grass, cutting brush and other general maintenance jobs. He had worked there a few weeks and told me that the foreman said they were looking to hire a couple more workers and thought maybe I should apply if I was interested. I told him I'd give it some thought.

A day or so passed and I decided I'd look into the job with the developers.

I pulled into the office drive and there was a flurry of vehicles raising dust as they drove across the highway and onto the dirt roads leading to the development property. There was a speaker on the side of the building with loud music annoyingly blasting away. Every so often, the music would stop, there would be an announcement about a lot being purchased and then the music would resume.

We Were Cowboys

I walked in the office door and was greeted by the receptionist who asked if she could help me.

Bernadette, as she was identified by the plastic nameplate on her desk, was thirtyish, at least that's what I thought, very attractive and had an actress's physique. Her dark hair was long, her tight skirt was short, exposing more than half of her stocking covered thigh and her perfume filled the room with a sweet, almost overpowering fragrance.

Momentarily distracted, I explained about the job opening and she told me to wait one moment as she left the room. Watching her leave, I sat down on a big green couch and began curiously looking at the office interior while I waited for the voluptuous secretary to return.

In a second or two, she returned to lead me down the hallway of the office and showed me to a room where a fellow wearing a big western hat was making all the announcements over the public address system.

"What can I help you with," he asked, pausing momentarily to speak into the microphone on the desk between us.

"I'm here to apply for the maintenance position."

He introduced himself, "I'm Larry. The job pays two dollars an hour. You can start tomorrow at seven a.m. Don't be late!"

Before I could say anything, we were interrupted by voices on the radio. He pulled a card from a big rack holding what appeared to be hundreds more, keyed the mic once more and hollered, "Sold," in a big boisterous voice as he placed the card in a different slot.

As quickly as it had started, the interview was over with a wave from him signaling me out the door.

It was ten minutes before seven when I pulled into the parking lot the following morning. Larry was handing out verbal instructions to two other guys I knew from high school. Finishing with them, he turned to me, re-introduced himself, handed me a chainsaw and told me to go with the other two guys,

"They will tell you what to do."

I hopped into the bed of the already running pick-up and they drove off into the bowels of the woods. I spent the next eight hours cutting brush off of fifty by one hundred foot camping lots, so prospective buyers could park a recreational vehicle on them. I did the same thing every day for the next few weeks. The work was hot and strenuous, so most that hired on did not stay long. I worked about a month and Robby and I were the only two workers left. Everyone else had quit.

Larry came in one morning, just as jovial as always, said we were going to start working on the old barn in the coming days. We were going to remodel it to make it a stable.

"It will have a dozen stalls. We'll bring in horses for the property owners and we can rent the extra stalls to the college girls from William Woods."

Along with the adjoining property, the development company had purchased the McClellan farm. A long since burnt house had sat on one side of the blacktopped road and the barn was on the other. The barn had been vacant since the house burnt and multiple seasons of weather and neglect had taken a heavy toll on the once thriving cattle barn. The rusty tin roof was still intact, but the side boards were weather worn badly and many were missing entirely.

At best, I thought this project would be a challenge for a couple teenagers.

Our duties shifted from primarily yard care to carpenters. For the next two months, board after board, nail after hundreds of nails and several buckets of paint, with help and guidance from Larry, we transformed the dilapidated pile of lumber and tin into a functional horse stables.

In a matter of a few weeks, Larry had procured four boarders and put me in charge of the daily care. He also told me I could keep my horse there as well, for partial payment for the extra work I'd be doing. It meant mucking stalls, feeding and watering each horse and generally keeping the place neat and orderly, duties I was glad to take on seven days a week.

I was working with horses on a daily basis, something I enjoyed immensely.

SHORTEST CATTLE DRIVE EVER

Carson caught me at Wright Brothers store fueling up my pickup. As he approached, he greeted me in his usual low voice and big smile. Although he was much older than me, he called me Mr. Baise most of the time.

"Good morning Mr. Baise, you doing good?"

I acknowledged his greeting as I completed the fueling process.

"I moved cows and calves off some rented ground down at Oscar Maddox and I wondered if you'd have time to run down and see if you could find one old lost cow. She might be dead for all I know, been gone a week."

I explained I couldn't go until the next day, but would be more than happy to do a search of the property in the morning.

Happy with my answer, he said he'd meet me about nine the next morning with a trailer. If I found her and was lucky enough to drive her to the corral, he would load her up and bring her home.

    I got up early the next morning to get everything ready to go look for the lost cow. I put a snack in my saddle bag, fed and groomed my horse, got the trailer hooked up and checked to ensure the lights were working properly. The temperature was warm, but the air was heavy with dew and that made it feel cooler than it actually was. I had pulled a light jacket on before leaving the house and was comfortable, I doubted I'd need the outer ware for long.

    Time slipped by faster than I had realized and I quickened my pace to get my horse tacked up. Once that was complete, I walked the saddled horse into the trailer and tied him to a D ring close to the front. Exiting the loaded trailer, I closed the end gate, which made a very audible noise in the morning haze and shrugged my shoulders to ward off a slight chill.

    I knew where the property was located, but had never been on it before. I also knew that it would probably be very rugged terrain and rocky most likely. A lot of the farms in the area had lots of big cedars growing on them and I figured this two-hundred-acre tract would be no different. This search could turn into a difficult one and it was quite possible that I might not locate the cow even if she was still alive.

We Were Cowboys

As I pulled down the long gravel drive, the trailer bounced from the potholes left by years of un-maintained service. I noticed Carson had made it before me. With his usual big smile and a "good morning," he began to explain the surrounding landscape.

My premonitions about the rocks and cedar trees were dead on, I couldn't see more than twenty feet in any direction and the steep hillside I had parked my rig on was littered with pretty good sized flintstones.

Carson continued by showing me the path that led to the interior of the heavily wooded farm and told me that would be the easiest way to gain access to the major portion of the acreage. Completing his instructions, Carson added he would stick around for an hour or two and if I hadn't shown back before then he would leave for home. I was to stop by his house if I got her penned up.

I opened the trailer gate and unloaded the horse I'd brought, tightened the cinch and mounted to begin my search and rescue mission. Carson held the pasture gate open and bid me a good morning as I trotted the gelding past him. I heard the gate close and latch behind me as I slowed the gelding to a walk. I didn't want to wear him out right away because we might be a while.

The path was very steep, had washed out ruts running its length, or at least as far as I could see and was beginning to be overgrown with brush and multi-floral rose bushes. The loose rock rolled under the horses' hooves with each step he took making him slip occasionally. Negotiating around the deepest ruts and attempting to avoid as much of the thorny rose bushes as possible was going to make for a long day in the saddle.

Concentrating to keep good footing, my horse suddenly threw his ears forward and very briefly stalled. I looked into the distance to see a black cow ascending the hill. With little to no place to get off the trail, I pulled slightly on the reins bringing the horse to a complete stop and stayed quiet to let the cow pass if she would. She too paused, identified what was approaching her and then slowly resumed her climb. I let her walk past and get a few feet ahead of me, then reined my horse around to keep her moving closer to the corral next to where I had entered the pasture.

Carson and Oscar were still standing next to the pasture gate and had not heard or seen me approaching. I let out a short, loud whistle giving them quite a surprise. Hurriedly, Oscar slipped through the fence and opened the corral gate allowing the once lost cow to enter. Once she had walked into the pen, Carson pulled a small pail of ground milo from the pickup bed and poured a little bit in the trough. There was more than enough grass in the pasture to keep one cow fed, but this ole gal was hogging down on the grain she had been given, like she hadn't eaten in weeks.

Still sitting on my cow pony, Carson told me "That didn't take long."

As I dismounted, I explained to him how the cow was already coming up the rocky hill when I encountered her.

"You want help loading her up?"

"Oh I don't think so, Oscar ain't got nothing better to do, he can help. What do I owe you for your time?"

"Carson you don't owe me a dime. I was glad I was able to help."

"Well, I sure appreciate it. I'll help you with something if you need it, Okay?"

"That will be payment good enough Carson," as I opened the end gate of the trailer and jumped the horse in.

By the time I got turned around and started back out the drive, the black cow was already loading in Carson's trailer. I suspect she had spent enough time alone and was ready to be back with her herd of cow friends.

Eddie Baise

THE RED ROAN

Ray asked if I'd ride his filly for thirty days. He offered one hundred bucks if I'd be willing to take the job. Dollar signs flashed before my young eyes and I jumped at the chance to make a hundred dollars. Gas was about thirty-six cents a gallon and that money would go a long ways for transportation. We made arrangements to get the two-year-old to the barn so I could start working her in the next few days.

The little roan stood about thirteen and a half hands, out of an Appaloosa mare and a smooth mouth sorrel stallion Ray's brother-in-law had raised from a colt, neither being of good conformation or disposition. Nervous from being displaced from her familiar surrounds, the filly shivered and blew from her nostrils with every step she took as I walked her to the stall I was going to keep her in. I decided I'd hold off tacking her up until the next morning so she might settle into her new temporary home.

Morning came and I began feeding and chores. As I headed to the new filly's stall, I heard a low nicker and thought maybe she had leveled out a bit overnight. I continued chores and after mucking all the stalls, I figured now was as good a time as any. I slung a halter over my shoulder and proceeded to my next month's project.

She shied just a little, but wasn't difficult to halter and I brought her around to the hitch rail to start sacking her out.

Simply picking up a saddle pad and one would have thought I'd tried to kill her. She jumped sideways, pulled against the lead and in a few moments she came back forward, then stood trembling. I implemented a little less speed and continued holding the blanket up to her until she accepted it without trying to run off.

Next, I would introduce the saddle. Once again she resisted, but with time and repeated attempts, I managed to get the saddle on her back. Not wanting to force too much on her at one time, I did not cinch her up and stopped for the time being.

Later that same day, I decided to try and tack her up to see if she had retained anything from the mornings' lesson. With a little re-schooling, she allowed me to put the saddle over her back. Facing forward, I reached under her belly and grabbed hold of the girth hanging from the off side. Careful not allowing it to touch her underside, I looped the cinch strap through the D ring of the girth. Now, I began slowly drawing the girth ever closer to the filly's nervous body until it just touched the red hair of her belly with no reaction to speak of. I made one more loop through the girth's ring and pulled with enough force to put a fair amount of pressure on the little horse. Her ears pinned in an instant and pulled back on the rope I'd tied to the rail. I let her pull on the rope for a little bit and she dove forward releasing the pressure she'd placed on the halter, then she pulled back once more.

I could tell this bomb was going to blow, so I un-knotted the rope and pulled the cinch strap tighter on her sweaty belly so I could see how far the shrapnel was going to fly. It scattered everywhere!

I held onto the lead for as long as I could and knowing she could not get out of the barns' alley, I finally let her go. The dust was so thick in a matter of no time, I could hardly see what the heck was happening. I could hear her bucking and groaning trying to rid herself of that awful piece of leather I'd strapped to her back.

Several days of this same routine and the dollar signs had been replaced with question marks, what the dickens had I gotten into?

On the sixth or seventh day, my youthful impatience gave in. I'd had enough of this patty cake treatment and felt it was time to crawl on top this mustang. I'd been getting her used to a snaffle bit from day one, so bridling was no issue and on this day she stood without bucking while being saddled. Was I getting through to her at long last?

After saddling up without incident, we headed to the corral for the big moment. The look in her eye told me she was not going to take to this without a fight. I pulled her head around to her left shoulder, put a boot in the stirrup, a hand on the horn, slung a leg over the saddle and braced for her to buck. She locked all four legs and stood dead still until I asked for forward motion. I got plenty of motion when I poked her sides with the spurs on my boots. Time and time again, I'd get mounted and she would buck until I was sent sprawling to the ground.

The dust I was creating each time I hit the dirt had long since turned to mud by the sweat generated from my bruised and battered body. I was young, wiry and thought I could rip a limb off a peach tree and whip a six-hundred-pound grizzly until he cried "uncle," but this little red roan horse was giving me an abusing workout. One I'd feel for days.

Two-thirds of the way through this month-long endeavor, I was able to saddle up and ride off without any bucking or blowing, but she still resisted any and all cues. She would not turn, stop, or back without fighting first. Only a few more days and I'd collect my hundred dollars.

On day thirty, I could not ride in the morning and had put it off until later that afternoon. When I did come in to saddle up and ride the outlaw filly, she was gone. I looked around and she wasn't in any of the stalls or out to pasture. Knowing how Ray was, I concluded he had come and got her. I was sure he felt if the horse was there more than a month, he'd owe me additional money.

I drove down to his house and sure enough, the roan was standing in the pasture by the house. Ray came out and I asked him about the horse. I was not prepared for the lecture I encountered and before he got finished with me, I felt like a schoolboy being scolded by the teacher.

Apparently, he saddled his red roan horse and was going to ride her home. He barely got out the gate, she got to moving too fast for him and he hauled back on the reins, pulling her over.

I pleaded had he told me he was going to take the mare, I would have explained her habits and that maybe the bit he was going to use was too harsh for her at this time of her training. He reluctantly handed me five twenties and told me I'd never ride one of his horses again.

To my knowledge, he never had another horse, never rode the red roan again and I think he finally hauled her to the sale barn.

We Were Cowboys

One hundred dollars was a considerable amount of money for a teenage kid to accumulate in thirty days. If I had thought the project through a bit longer considering the feed, the stall cleaning, the wear and tear on my equipment and the beating I took, I would have held out for another hundred. I guess, sometimes some lessons come a little harder than others. The hard ones though, you remember a whole lot longer than the ones that come easy.

WILD COW MILKING

Robby and I were asked to help gather livestock to put in a rodeo for the coming weekend. We were to go down to the Bison-Aire and meet up with Henry, the ranch boss. He'd get us lined out.

The Bison-Aire was a five thousand acre ranch near Williamsburg, that was owned by some city slicker out of St. Louis. It looked just about like pictures I had seen of southwest Texas. Rocks and buck brush were the only things coming out of the ground, the place was nearly barren in some areas and the land was bone poor.

There were several species of exotic animals that weren't normally seen on a working cattle ranch, only in a zoo. There were zebras, giraffes, and buffalo, to mention just a few. Most of these animals were very wild and weren't accustomed to seeing people on a regular basis. Henry cautioned us wanna-be-cowboys to stay clear of those particular pens.

We Were Cowboys

We caught up with the boss and got our instructions. We jumped our mounts in the back of an old rusted up trailer to haul to the back side of the ranch. Henry was driving the truck, dragging the trailer across several little creeks dried up by the summer heat. The whole time we were moving, he was hollering instructions over the noise of the truck and where he thought the cows might be. We got back to the designated area of the ranch and sure enough, he's right. However, with the noise of that truck and trailer banging through the burnt-up pastures, the cows raised their tails and scattered like mice running out of the corn crib.

We spent five, or possibly six hours trying to round up enough cows for the wild cow milking event. Finally, there were seven or eight cows and a few calves in the lot that we could load in the rattletrap trailer to bring back to the pens on the house side of the ranch.

The Boss loaded the cows and left the calves. Robby and I were told to turn the remaining calves out and ride back to the main house. I questioned Henry about the calves and the cows being separate and was told they would be able to "mama-up" after the weekend event.

We spent the next day getting the bulls up, a much easier task. With the heat as it was, the bulls didn't want to run unless you crowded them pretty hard, so we didn't bother them much. A couple of them had pretty nasty horns and attitudes to match. If one of us or our mounts had gotten hooked by one of the bulls' horns, it could have been a disastrous end to human or horse.

After gathering the bulls, Henry decided he wanted to see if this lot of bulls we had gathered would buck. This batch of stock wasn't pro rodeo stock, they were true wild stock right off the range and had never been handled, except for vaccinations. The boss told us to load a few bulls in the chutes and we'd see what they would do. He said Robby and I could buck a couple of them out if we wanted.

Neither, Robby nor I had ever been on a bull, but when my friend said he'd do it, I was going to ride a bull too. Henry gave both of us a quick lesson in "holdin' on" and the next thing I knew, I had my skinny little, one hundred-twenty pound butt sitting right square on top of a half-ton of mad bovine. Henry was laughing robustly the whole time when he turned the bull and me out of the chute. About four good jumps and I was tossed into the air. I came down at the speed of light, crashing into the dirt and manure.

"That one will do!" he barks and we run one through for Robby.

Robby and I took turns bucking out two or three apiece before Henry decided he had enough good bulls for the coming buck off.

The first evening of the rodeo was going well. We got the bareback and the saddle broncs all run

We Were Cowboys

through and we were going to let the pick-up horses rest a spell.

The announcer proclaims, "Its' time for the wild cow milking,"

Anyone wanting a chance to win fifteen dollars could put a dollar in the hat to have a go at it.

Three people were to make a team, one heading, one on the tail and one milking. You had to surround the cow and get enough milk in a cup to display it to the judge.

Robby, Bryce and I teamed up. The two of them elected me to be the milker. That decision was made because they thought I wasn't big enough to hold a cow. I decided that was a fair plan because I didn't feel like butting heads with a wild cow and I sure didn't want to be on the tail end of a mad wild cow that was still looking for her baby.

Everyone got lined up across the arena.

"Three—two—one—turn 'em loose."

All those cows had been penned away from the calves for two or three days and they weren't happy about it at all. When they came through the gates, they were looking for those calves of theirs. I'd never seen so many people scatter so fast in all my life. The cows cleared the arena in just a few moments. The crowd went crazy with laughter, it was quite the spectacle for a while.

After a short while, a few of us "brave" cowboys hopped back over the arena fence in an attempt to get that little prized dab of milk. Two or three teams were able to get a rope on a cow, but couldn't manage to hang on. It took us a good ten minutes to get our cow held up enough to get one or two little squirts in the cup.

After I got the milk, I was supposed to run to the judge where ever he might be and pour the milk out to prove I had gotten it.

Squirt, squirt and I was off, but much to my dismay, another team had lucked out and the milker was about 4 strides ahead of me and displayed his bounty first. It didn't matter though. For me, it was all in fun.

MOTORCYCLE RIDE

Although our hearts were very deeply rooted in horses, working cattle on the ranch and the ways of the cowboy, as teenagers, our interests varied from season to season. Sometimes, more often than that.

Much to the dislike of his dad, Robby had bought a motorcycle from one of his older family friends. This motorcycle was a Suzuki 250 and when I saw this fine piece of motorized equipment for the first time, I thought it looked like a pile of junk. It was all rusted up, tires all weather cracked and just a partially assembled mess.

Summer was coming up, so we decided to take this thing apart, paint it and fix it all up, then reassemble it.

I had a 350 Honda at the time and we figured if we put our efforts together, we could get that Suzuki running and then ride together much sooner.

Eddie Baise

He tore into the thing and pulled it all apart. He then started sanding on the tank and fenders to get them all painted up.

When he purchased the Suzuki, it had fourth gear out of it and you had to double shift at that point to get into 5th gear. Neither, he nor I knew how to fix it so it would shift right, so we left the transmission alone. Bad transmission and all, we decided we're going go one get this thing on the road.

We got the bike all painted up, put back together and we were going to take it to Wilson's Garage in Williamsburg to get it inspected. Robby poured a little gas in the tank, pumped the kick starter and took off down the driveway, then turned to the south. We were going to cut through the woods on the gravel to stay off the main roads. That way, if we had trouble, we could walk back, plus, Robby didn't have a motorcycle license.

Robby was in front and I was behind on my bike as he took off like a cat that had turpentine wiped on its backside, just shifting through the gears. The old road we were on, was surely laid out by a snake because it was as crooked as the devil. He was cranking the throttle and shifting through the gears like he was crazy. The next thing I knew, he ran off the corner of the road near Gibbs lane.

The motorcycle ran down in the ditch making dust fly, hit a rut and started flipping through the air. I saw Robby go flying high into the air, landing face down in the weeds. I figured the worst had just happened to my friend right before my eyes. By the time I got my motorcycle shut down and got to where Robby was laying, he was moaning, groaning and cussing, ··Yes, he was still living, but I could hardly believe it.

After a few minutes, Robby got up and I was checking him out to see how bad he was hurt. He just had the wind knocked out of him and a little scratch on his wrist. The bike, however, didn't fare so well though.

The smell of gasoline put me on alert, thinking this whole mess might catch fire at any moment. We began to look for all the parts that slung off the wrecked bike and Robby was thinking we could re-attach the recovered parts to finish our road trip to Williamsburg. Very soon though, we both realized that wasn't going to happen. The seat flew one way, the fuel tank another, the handlebars were bent, both mirrors were knocked off and there was a flat tire to top off the list of damaged equipment.

We both set on the side of the road for a minute or two trying to figure out what to do next. We didn't have long to figure though because Robby's dad showed up. We hadn't gone more than a half mile from the house and Bob had heard all the motorcycle noises come to an end. Concerned about Robby's welfare, he came to see what had happened.

After a good "I told you so" scolding, we loaded the Suzuki up in the back of the half-ton pickup and hauled it back to the barn where the pieces were piled in a corner.

A few days later, Robby asked if he could borrow my 350 cc motorbike to visit his girlfriend down the road. (Same road) It was probably 10 pm or later and I thought pretty hard about not loaning him my ride, but finally, I gave him the green light, --it was his girlfriend after all!

It seemed like he was gone forever. When he finally did come riding up, he was skint from head to toe.

"What the heck happened now?" I asked.

He explained as he was headed to his destination, he hit one of the neighbors' cows that had gotten out. The damage to my Honda was extensive, but I was able to get it restored using salvaged parts.

Robby was a pretty good cowboy and could ride just about any horse he encountered, but he couldn't ride a motorcycle worth a darn.

We Were Cowboys

KAWASAKI 900 Z1

Robby hadn't any more than wrecked his bike until he was thinking about another one. The ole Suzuki lay in the barn in pieces with little hope of us putting it back together. All summer he would ride mine or someone else's if they would let him.

Robby had a desire to ride motorcycles, but was hindered by not owning a good bike that would run and his inability to control one very well.

As fall came, the weather got cooler and the season for motorcycle riding was coming to a close. He bought a couple cycle magazines, looked at all the pictures, read the articles and dreamed of buying this motorcycle or that one. One evening late, he called me and said he had something cool to show me.

The next day, he brought one of the magazines to school to show me this motorcycle showcased in an article.

It was the Kawasaki 900 cc Z 1. This was an in-line four-cylinder beauty, rated one of the fastest production motorcycles of the time, with a top speed of 130 mph. Robby decided this was the bike he was going to own.

The price tag on these motorcycles was a shade over $2000 and he began to save his money to buy one. As time went on, he collected more money and came up with this idea that I should trade my Honda plus some boot and get one of the 900's also. I thought this was a grand idea and began my own campaign to save money.

Bucking hay, cutting cedar, saving lunch money and me working weekends at the filling station, our nest eggs were beginning to grow. Fall became winter, winter to spring and we were almost ready to go pick out our new rides. Just a few more skipped lunches at school and we would be there.

We finally decided we had saved enough money to make a purchase, so we were going to see what kind of deal we could make. We had it figured if we bought 2 bikes at one time, we might get a better price.

We made a plan for me to spend the night and the next morning we would head to the dealership in Columbia to check out the motorcycles. We stayed up late lying around watching TV and just hanging out.

Morning rolled around and Edith hollered "Breakfast."

We Were Cowboys

I got up first, then Robby and we went to the kitchen where Edith had bacon, eggs, homemade biscuits and gravy waiting. We dug in and ate until we were about to pop. After finishing her meal, Edith headed to the living room, retired to her recliner, dug out her cigarette machine and began rolling her home-rolled cigarettes while the dishes were cleaned up by Robby and me.

We got the kitchen straightened up, then went into Robby's room to collect our jackets for our trip to Columbia. We rounded the hall corner and Edith asked where we are headed in such a hurry. Robby told her we're headed to Columbia, but did not reveal our entire plan.

"Well you can go to Columbia, but you're not going to buy any motorcycle over there," she said.

Robby and I looked at each other, with that "oh-no" look and knew our plan is out in the open. We hadn't really tried to keep it secret, we just hadn't told anyone.

She explained she had seen the open magazine while cleaning Robby's room and read enough of the article to decide her son was not going to ride a motorcycle, especially one that would run 130 miles per hour.

Robby began to plead his case, but his mom would have nothing to do with it. I sat down on the couch keeping my mouth shut and let the two of them argue. He saw she was not going to cave, so he rested his case.

Eddie Baise

Edith lite a cigarette, took a long draw and turned to me.

"You're not buying one either!" she proclaimed. "And what were you thinking? He's wrecked your motorcycle twice and you're going to encourage him to buy something like that?"

I sank down into the couch cushions as far as I could and didn't say a word. She wasn't my mother, but I had spent just about as much time there as my own home and I wasn't about to cross her or disrespect her either.

She took another puff off the cigarette and went back to rolling more. Robby and I laid around for the rest of the day like a couple whipped pups.

About two weeks had passed and I was to meet Robby at his house one evening. I drove down the lane and Robby wasn't there yet, so I went in the house. Edith was sitting in the recliner rolling cigarettes and welcomed me in. The TV was on, so I sat down on the couch and listened to it for a few minutes before Edith asked what we were up to for the night. I told her we both had dates and was going to the King-Cal drive in. She went on to ask if either one of us had been looking at motorcycles after she had told us we weren't going to buy those 900 Kawasaki's. We had not, I told her so and that we had decided we would save our money for something else, maybe a really good cutting horse. She thought that was a good idea and told me

We Were Cowboys

neither of us needed one of those fast motorcycles because we would surely get hurt or worse.

Robby talked about the Kawasaki for several weeks, but neither of us ever looked at one.

It was probably a good thing we didn't.

TWENTY BUCKS THE HARD WAY

    One Friday evening, Bryce, Robby and I headed down to Raleigh Lederman's place in Rhineland to trim some horses. Raleigh was an old horse trader and had come up with a handful of two-year-olds from southern Missouri he wanted to get cleaned up for resale. He favored Appaloosa horses but would buy anything he thought he could turn a dollar or two on. This herd happened to be mostly quarter types, with one or two of mixed breed.

    Raleigh had called on us a couple other times before, so we knew there might be some trouble handling any or all of them. Bryce had made all the arrangements with Raleigh, so neither Robby nor I knew how many we might be doing, but we knew we would get ten dollars a head for each one we trimmed.

We Were Cowboys

We got down to the barn about seven, met up with Raleigh and went to inspect the horses that were to be worked on. As luck would have it, there was only six head to be done, but none of them had ever had a halter on. We chatted for a little bit, Raleigh said he had to go and we figured we had better get started. We took a little time and each one of us decided which horse we would work on.

This stall barn was about two hundred feet long, with stalls on both sides of a narrow, ten-foot alley. Each horse had a separate stall, which was only ten foot by ten foot, so catching should be easy, holding on however, might not be so easy.

The plan was to get a horse caught, get a halter on him, get him out of the stall and snubbed up to a post in the hallway. It sounded like the perfect plan. We found out rather quickly there was no perfect plan when it came to working these two-year-olds.

I grabbed a halter, unbuckled it, stuck the loose end in my mouth and slid open the stall door. I eased up to this little bay and got a hand on one shoulder, just waiting for him to bolt. He didn't. I got an arm around his neck, grabbed the loose end of the halter with my hand, then very carefully slipped it over his nose and got it buckled. I figured this was a good time to let him rest and for me to relax. Resting wasn't on his mind and relaxing was out of the question for me. The little bay had seen the open stall door and had been waiting for the right moment to bust loose. He bolted and tried to run past me, but I was able to keep one hand over his nose and an arm around his neck. However, he made it through the narrow opening with me hanging on. It was a good thing both of us were pretty skinny because the pair of us hit both sides of the doorway as we went out. Down the hallway we went, running into everything sticking out. We made it to one end of the alley and turned to go the next direction in very much the same manner. My feet were only hitting the ground about every twenty-five yards or so.

Bryce heard all the commotion we were making and headed my way to lend a helping hand. Throwing up his hands in front of the wild bronc, Bryce got him shut down long enough for me to regain some small amount of breath and a better grip. Back the other way we went, me flapping in the wind like a towel on the clothesline and the colt blowing and bouncing side to side down the alley.

I was thinking this colt is going to have to stop pretty soon because I was running out of hide to leave on the rough sawn oak stall fronts. We made it about halfway to the end of the alley when the little bay tuckered out long enough for me to get him snubbed.

After a short breather, I got under the colt and started trimming his feet. He didn't care too much for it, but he was too tired to fight very much. After a couple hours, I had one of my two finished.

We Were Cowboys

Robby and Bryce were having their own troubles with the colts they were working on. They had changed their minds about letting the horse out of the stall, so those fights were fairly well under control.

I figured I had better start on my second colt because they were already working on their second horse. Although this next colt was harder to catch, I did a little better at keeping her in the stall. We banged around for a little bit and I was able to get this one snubbed without any help. However, this sorrel filly wanted no part of me fiddling with her feet.

The first horse had skint me up pretty well and I had done everything I could to get this filly trimmed without getting killed. After finishing with her, I only had one toe smashed and one big bruise on my thigh where she had kicked me.

We finished up a little before midnight and headed home. As Bryce was driving, we were recalling our evening adventures over a cold beverage, one was bragging about how bad his horse was, or how one of us had handled our horse better than the other. But we all agreed on one thing. That was twenty bucks, the hard way.

Eddie Baise

FALL ROUND-UP

I shut the truck off and headed to the barn. As I rounded the corner, I was reminded by the hungry horses stalled there, I was late. Only ten minutes, but when a horse's time clock goes off, they know it's time to eat. A few minutes into my chores, I slipped back out to the pickup and dug behind the seat in search of another layer. I hadn't expected it to be so cool and the cold air was going right through me. Down under a collection of old dirty t-shirts left over from the summer, I found my Levi jacket. By appearances, it had been hidden for quite some time, so I attempted to shake at least a little dust off the wrinkled fabric. As I forced one arm into the wadded-up sleeve and then the other, I hoped something bad hadn't taken up residence. I turned up the collar to block the cold breeze and my mind was put to rest about anything living anywhere near that pile of blue jean cloth, although, it did smell like something had died in it

We Were Cowboys

at some point. Returning to the barn, I finished up my chores.

I was getting ready to go to the Bison-Aire to help gather stock to be vaccinated, so I brushed out the young mare I was going to use and got her saddled. I knew Robby was probably waiting for me to pick him up, so I hurriedly got the trailer hooked up, loaded the mare and headed just a mile or so down the road. Robby was just finishing tacking up a gelding he'd bought some time ago as I pulled in the drive. Leaving the engine running, I went around back, opened the end gate and Robby's mount walked in beside my mare. He asked if I wanted a cup of coffee for the road and motioned me toward the house trailer. Two cups of coffee, out the door and we were headed to Williamsburg.

When we got to the ranch, Henry pointed toward the east and motioned us where to park our rig. Robby and I bailed out of the truck, walked around back to unload and we could hear Henry barking orders to a couple of the other hands that were there to help. I drew the cinch up tight and the mare humped her back. I was thinking there might be a little rodeo on that morning and patted the half app on the neck, hoping she'd relax a bit before I mounted.

Henry spouted out the plan for the round-up and told everyone to mount up. My mares back hadn't gone down much, but she did not buck when I slung my leg over the saddle. We headed northeast, past the buffalo pens and on down to the creek where the cows were supposed to be. The blackberry vines and multi-floral rose bushes were pretty thick and the young mare had to carefully pick her way through as we searched for the herd. The sun had been replaced by a heavy layer of clouds and it looked like rain. The smelly Levi jacket was barely enough to ward off the shivers, but the search continued.

One of the cowboys had located a group of twenty or more cows and three or four bulls and motioned to the rest of us the direction we needed to be in order to move the herd towards the corrals.

All the cattle on the Bison-Aire were fairly wild and weren't used to being pushed around, so to have any success at getting the herd corralled meant taking extra time and giving them plenty of space. Once we got close to the pens, we would go through a set of gates and then close them behind us. Each set of gates meant we were in a smaller pen. After three hours at a slow, steady pace, we had the whole herd in the smallest pen and then all we had to do was push them into the alley that led to the squeeze chute.

Henry had me stay in the small pen to push the herd into the alley. The alley was wide on the open end, narrowed down as it got closer to the head chute and long enough for five or six cows to crowd into.

We Were Cowboys

All was going well until one of the bulls decided it wasn't his turn to go down the alley. I'd kept the herd moving and headed for the narrow end of the pen, but each time this ole bull got near the opening, he'd force his way out of the bunch. Each time he busted out, he'd scatter the herd and I'd have to push them back to the alley.

My young mare wasn't much of a cow horse, so I was pulling and tugging on her head the entire time. On one occasion, the angry bull challenged us and the mare hadn't a clue she and I were about to get run over. I buried the cheap store-bought spurs into her rib cage and swatted her backside with the leather reins making her hop a couple times, but eluded the unruly charging bull.

Henry had Robby mount up once more to help me with the angry critter. Robby's horse had more cow sense and a three-hundred-pound advantage on my mare. With the help of an extra hand, the bull finally gave in and got in line in the alley. However, he was not at all content to remain in line and began throwing a fit. Before he was done, he had run over two cows, under one, turning her up-side-down in the alley and flew through the head chute. With a flurry of profanities Henry told us to let him go. The last time we saw him, he was headed north at a high rate of speed and the rickety old fences weren't enough to stop him.

Eddie Baise

We finished the last few that had been upset in the alley and opened the gates, turning the herd back out to the wild.

Our ride back to the truck was filled with laughter and comments about the rogue bull and where he might end up. Henry made some comment about the bull ending up in the freezer if he ever saw him again.

SURPRISINGLY SHOCKED

The weather had turned really cold for a few days and the water pipe at the barn had frozen. Unable to water the horses, I asked Larry, the stable manager, if we should get a heat tape and wrap the pipe up with hopes of it thawing out soon. Open flame was not an option for fear of setting the whole place ablaze. He agreed and set off for Calwood to purchase the appropriate equipment. While he was gone I continued my chores of cleaning stalls and turning out horses that were to be on pasture for the day.

Larry returned from the store with a heat tape, an extension cord and a roll of duct tape, along with verbal instructions on how he wanted the job completed. I questioned the instructions but was informed that this was how he wanted it done. I complied with the orders as he had given them and turned the power on to the tape hoping to have water in a short time. The quick fix worked in short order and I watered before leaving to complete other work that needed to be taken care of.

The heat tape had an auto shutoff, and if the temperature was above forty degrees, the chore of plugging and unplugging was not necessary, so no one really paid much attention to it. Because the location of the water spigot was next to the alley wall, it was handy for the boarders to tie their horses in cross ties to bathe them.

On one warmer day, Sue, one of the college women boarding her horse there, tied her full-blooded appaloosa gelding to one of the cross ties in preparation to give him a bath. I was cleaning a stall while she and I chatted about how warm the morning was and how nice a day had been forecast. Sue went into the tack room gathering her supplies and the gelding was playing with the cross tie in his lips.

After a little bit, I heard an unusual sound and poked my head out of the stall, looking in the direction of the noise. To my astonishment I saw the gelding had the extension cord in his mouth. A quick visual told me the gelding had played with the cord leading to the heat tape and had broken the protective insulation.

With his eyes rolled back, his body leaning slightly back, legs locked and quivering, I surmised the horse was being electrocuted. Remembering lessons from my dad about what to do in the case of electrical shock, I ran for the end of the cord where it was plugged into the wall. With a quick jerk the power was cut from the faulty cord, releasing the horse from the one hundred-twenty-volt death grip. The gelding stood up straight, shook his head, blinked his eyes and then licked his lips.

Rather quickly, Sue had discovered something was going on and with her sleepy New Jersey drawl asked what had happened. As I tied the dazed horse to a different cross tie, I explained the event as I had seen it. She thanked me for saving her horse from certain death and suggested the power cord should be relocated to a safer position.

Unable to reposition the power cord, I made a makeshift cover and moved the cross ties so another horse couldn't duplicate the near-death experience of the Appaloosa gelding.

Sue finished grooming her horse and decided to go for a short ride around the nearby lake. She was gone less than an hour and on her return, I asked how her ride went.

"Oh my," she said, "He sure was full of energy today!!"

Not realizing what she had just said, I gave her a nod and just chuckled to myself.

Eddie Baise

LESSONS FOR AN UN-BROKE COLT

I mounted my horse, looped the lead I was holding to the horn and snubbed the un-broke colt close. I didn't tie off tight in the event the colt I was to pony blew a gasket. I got settled in and told Robby I was ready. In one swift motion, he stuck his boot in the stirrup and swung his leg over the young horse's back. The wiry colt was already in motion before Robby's right-hand boot hit the off side stirrup, but he was able to stay aboard. The wide-eyed colt made one lunge forward and locked up.

Robby got collected and we sat motionless for a minute or so to let this little sorrel "think about it". Robby tipped his head and I cautiously urged my horse forward, bracing for a possible wreck. I had never ponied another horse with this mare and I wasn't at all sure how she might react to the extra

We Were Cowboys

pressure from the girt on her belly. She momentarily staggered as the colt resisted, but leaned into the breast collar and kept pulling. The colt continued to pull and resist moving forward. Each time the lead would tighten, he would crow hop instead of willingly walking beside the pony.

Once the unwilling colt began to buck, I quickly turned and spurred the mare forward, pulling him around and off balance, hoping he would not un-seat his rider. The rope dug into my leg, slipping slightly in my hand. Despite the burns the moving rope created, I was able to maintain my grip.

Once again, the colt stopped and we let him settle. We set nearly two minutes before the colt began to lick his lips and in a bit more he unlocked and shifted his weight to three legs. After a little while longer, Robby applied a bit of leg pressure to encourage forward motion and there was initial resistance, but eventually, the colt moved out. We would walk a ways and the little crooked-legged horse would try hopping again. On down the highway right-a-way towards Toledo we moved. About a mile and a half of the half-hearted bucking and trying to pull away from the pony horse and the colt was beginning to breathe pretty heavy. However, with each yard we went, he resisted less.

By the time we hit the junction and headed to Broken Bridge, the four of us were all sweated up. We stopped to rest and discussed removing the lead to see if the colt would follow on his own. I handed the rope to Robby and nudged the mare down the road with the colt setting in behind her right away.

We got down to the creek and let our mounts have a well-deserved drink of the cool water. We piddled around for a while, thinking about which route we should take back to the house to prevent over-doing this colt on his first outing. After the horses seemingly quenched their thirst, we made our way back up the hill by the old thrasher and out onto the right-a-way once again. From there we only had a mile or so of fairly easy traveling to get back to the barn.

At a slow pace, we made it back to the barn, slid the saddles off the sweat-drenched horses, brushed them down and turned them out in the lot. As usual, the horses both found a dust pile and rolled, covering their hide with a thick coat of red dirt, soaking up the excess moisture. Up, they came, shaking the fine powder loose, which created a cloud that glistened in the bright afternoon sun as they ran off in the direction of the other horses.

LARRY IS GONE ON VACATION

The summer had progressed well. The stables had four college women keeping their horses there for the summer, Robby and I both had our horses there and Larry had bought a pair of Appaloosa geldings as well. There was almost always someone at the barn riding, grooming, or just hanging out.

Robby had been assigned mounted security, which was nothing more than riding around the project greeting people to see if they needed anything or checking to see that any equipment left parked hadn't been vandalized. I stayed busy at the barn, keeping that area cleaned up and I also had to keep the grass at the office cut. Larry came and went pretty much as he pleased and I never knew when he might be around on any given day, but he showed every day.

Fall was setting in, daylight was getting shorter and things had come to a halt as far as the development company selling lots or any equipment running. All of the salespeople were gone, as was the receptionist. The only ones left were Larry, Robby and me.

Larry and I worked through the winter months keeping everything going that needed attention, but it didn't take much to maintain the project grounds. Robby wasn't doing security any longer and Larry would come in long enough to send in the weeks' payroll. We weren't really putting in forty hours anymore, but we were getting forty hours pay. Larry laid Robby off right after Christmas and I thought I'd be gone anytime soon, but somehow it didn't happen.

One Friday, just about time grass was beginning to green up, Larry told me that he and his wife were going on vacation for a while. Payroll had been turned in and I'd get my check just like always the next week. He left another week's payroll application lying on the desk and I was to turn that one into corporate in California the following Friday.

It was very quiet working alone. It didn't take long to do what was needed each day and when I would finish, I would go to the office to watch television until it was time to chore once more in the evening.

The next Friday came around, I sent the paperwork in as instructed and just as Larry had stated, a check came midway through the following week like they had for several months.

Two weeks had passed, it was Monday morning and I fully expected Larry to roll in anytime as he had for months. He did not. He didn't come in any of that week and on Friday I was wondering what to do about turning in my hours. I dug around on Larry's desk and found another signed form. I copied it on the fax machine and sent it off.

One morning, I was doing chores at the stables and a car I didn't recognize pulled in the drive. An older gentleman got out, came in the hallway of the barn and introduced himself. I knew him from the lumber yard where Dad had bought lumber several times.

"Eddie, is Larry around?"

"No sir, Larry's gone on vacation."

"He is. You know when he'll be back?"

"No sir, he just said he was going on vacation. I really figured he'd be back by now, but I haven't seen him for a couple weeks now."

The gentleman volunteered that Larry had charged a fair amount of the building material at his lumber yard and the bill was overdue.

"If you see Larry, tell him to call me or come by. Will you?"

"Yes sir, I will."

He turned, entered his automobile and drove away.

On the fourth week of me turning in my own time, I immediately got a phone call. It was from corporate. I had conversed with the lady on the other end before and she was always pleasant to talk with. This time, however, she was frank and to the point.

"Who turned that time sheet in?"

I explained I had been making a copy of an old pay request in Larry's absence and forwarding it.

"You need to stop doing that. Larry does not work here any longer. You don't need to send anything. I'll send your checks each week. Stop sending any documents with Larry's signature on them. Is that understood?"

"Yes, Mam," and the line went dead.

I sat in the chair at the desk for minutes trying to collect myself. What in the world had happened? What was I supposed to do? What was going to happen with all the stuff the development company had here? Was the place shutting down? My young mind could not completely grasp what was going on.

I eventually surmised, possibly, Larry wasn't coming back, the company had pulled the plug on the project and either fired or moved everyone associated with it. I was the only one left and I didn't have a clue what to do. I decided since I was still getting paid, I would continue doing what I'd been doing for the last few months and wait to see what happened.

My plan seemed like a reasonable one, but it was flawed. First, I realized Larry had all the money the stable had been generating, if, in fact it was making any profit. Second, he was doing all the purchasing of the feed and supplies that were needed. I assumed with rent money from the boarders. Third, the electric and water were paid by the company and I had no idea how long that might continue. Fourth, I had no business experience at all. I was in trouble.

All this disaster hit near the end of the month. I knew rent was going to be coming in and I'd have at least enough money to cover feed. I talked all the tenants into paying with cash or making their checks payable to me instead of Larry. I had a little money left after purchasing enough feed to last two, maybe three weeks. What I didn't count on was the lumber yard owner showing back up. This time, he looked like he meant business.

Mr. Stack and I had a lengthy conversation about Larry's disappearance, the overdue bill, the development company, the stables where all his material was nailed together and the money the renters paid. I knew I was going to have to do the right thing.

"Mr. Stack, I have two hundred and sixty dollars this place has made. I know that isn't enough to cover the bill left by Larry. I don't feel that I am responsible for his bill, but that money is not mine. If I give you the money, the two hundred-sixty dollars, will that satisfy you?"

He lowered his head for a moment and then declared, "Apparently, I will never get any more from Larry, so yes, that will have to do. I appreciate your honesty."

We shook on the deal I had proposed and I gave him the money.

After writing Mr. Stack a check for the amount agreed upon, I was left with less than one hundred dollars of my own money in my account. I had a sick feeling in my gut. I couldn't keep the stables going on the small amount of rent money coming in each month, but I thought I could try.

Common sense overruled and told me I was fighting a losing battle, besides, this property and the barn wasn't even mine. I didn't know what the company was going to do and I had no money to operate on. I had to think more about this.

William Woods College would be ending classes in about a month and a half and all the boarders were students of the university. The morning after I paid off the debt owed by Larry, I told each girl at the end of the semester the barn would be closing. I explained the situation and that I was sorry for any inconveniences they might incur, but I felt I could not keep the stables going under the circumstances. It was a tough day because I'd worked so hard at something I enjoyed and I had learned valuable lessons as well. I matured a great deal in a short period of time.

Shortly after I moved the last of the tenants out of the barn, I received an envelope in the mail with a return address of California. I opened the parcel and it contained a letter and two checks. The letter was from corporate headquarters. It read:

Dear Mr. Baise,

Your services are no longer required. Your last week's check and one week of severance are enclosed.

Sincerely,

Lake Development LLC

Eddie Baise

MONEY ROUND

I can see the smoke of the bar-b-que pits in the damp night air. The smell is tempting, but I walk up to the table, hand a ten-dollar bill to the cashier and tell him my name. He scribbles on a tablet, opens a cigar box, pulls out a piece of paper and responds in a dull monotone voice, "Round one, bull five."

I turn and walk towards the chutes to wait.

My mind is whirling a million thoughts as I place my bag of gear on the ground near the fence, pull out my rope and hang it from the top rail next to another cowboy's. There is a sense of excitement, but most everyone is calm as they prepare their equipment.

One cowboy opens a pouch of Redman and places a big chew in his mouth, another has his hat off, head bowed, eyes closed, momentarily motionless and yet another kneels in the corner by the holding pens, straining to vomit, his nerves making him sick to his stomach.

We Were Cowboys

I grab my spurs, buckle them on my boots and continue to watch and wait.

The holding pen gates begin to swing and bulls are walking to their position, one after the other, six total. The cowboys are now gathering behind their perspective chutes scoping out their assigned ride. I have drawn a big gray with short curled horns and his eyes as black as coal.

Before long the announcer calls the first rider. Moments later the chute gate opens. I draw a single leather glove from the bag, pull it onto my right hand and tie it snug around my wrist with a leather lace.

One after the other a name is called and a chute gate opens and closes as the cowboys make their attempt to cover a bull. My heart begins to pound in my chest as my name is called. I look down into the chute and a wrangler tells me, "It's your turn."

I pull myself up over the chute, place a boot on each side and lower my bull rope beside the massive beast below me. The ground man hooks the bottom end and I hear the bell clanging as he pulls it up to me. I loop it together and draw it up just tight enough that it doesn't slip. A cowboy on my right grabs the tail end and I slide my gloved hand up and down the braided rope to heat the rosin, making it sticky to the touch. I place my hand, knuckles down, between the bull's dirty hide and the rope as the cowboy pulls with enough force to bury my knuckles deep into the muscled flesh. Clamping my fingers down on the rosined rope and a single wrap around my wrist, I push myself up over my hand and drop my legs beside the bull feeling him tense his every muscle. The bull is moving in anticipation and presses my leg so painfully tight against the chute, it feels as though the bones within could be crushed into tiny fragments at any point.

I hear someone ask if I'm ready. I pull my hat down tight with my free hand, nod I am, take in a breath and expel, "Outside," as the gateman pulls the gate latch.

With an explosion of dust, cowbell clanging and cowboy cheers, the bull exits the chute. He blows high into the air, jerking my head backward and pulling me slightly off my hand. I attempt to remain centered on the back of this fifteen-hundred-pound bull as he equally attempts to be rid of me. Looking right at the head of the bull anticipating his next move, I continue my fight with my spurs hooked deep into his rib cage, my hand grasping the rope with all my might. An eternity has passed and I question,

"Have I missed the buzzer, is it time to bail?"

Without warning, I'm catapulted high into the air in a series of uncontrolled flips. Time passes slowly and it seems I'm in the air longer than I was on the bull, but as quickly as I went up, I hit the ground landing on my hands and knees knowing I can't stay here long. Dulled senses make my movements seem such a monumental task at this point and before I can make it to my feet a clown has already got a hold on me, encouraging me to get up and move out.

Back on my own two wobbly legs now, I see the winner of this round headed to the gate leading to the holding pens. With the danger of being trampled or gored gone and knowing I didn't make the money round, I slowly walk back to the chute and hear the announcer making a remark,

"NO SCORE FOR THAT COWBOY."

One of the clowns walks towards me, hands me my bull rope, pats me on the shoulder and says "Better luck next time."

Once more, the fragrance of bar-b-que passes my nostrils luring me in the direction of the food stand.

Eddie Baise

A BUCKING APPALOOSA

I bought a half app filly one summer as a project horse. This college girl I knew needed money, I needed a horse. We came to terms on this flashy two-year-old horse and I brought her home. I began working on this pretty little horse and before long, she was doing very well. I had worked her for a while and thought having a trail ride the coming weekend would be a good time to get her used to long rides with other horses.

I invited several people on our ride but didn't know how many might show up, or if everyone that came would have a ride. If someone didn't have a horse, they would have to double up with another rider. Such was the case this weekend. One gal didn't have a horse so she was going to double with me.

I got the filly next to the wooden board fence and the young lady slid over on to the hips of the horse. I had not had another person with me on this horse and right away it was certain this might not work out. We stood there for a moment to let the filly relax and get used to the extra weight. Everything seemed to be okay, so I decided to move out just a little and size the situation up. In two steps it became apparent it wasn't going to work.

The little sorrel appaloosa blew up and started bucking. Then she reared, falling over backward. Fortunately, my passenger and I both were able to escape without any harm done to us. The horse, however, rolled on the ground for a bit finally getting to her feet. My saddle that was still tightly cinched to the horse got roughed up pretty bad.

The young lass decided to partner up with a more stable mount and I remounted this bucking bronc to begin our ride once more. Our ride lasted three or four hours without a hitch. She rode like she was a very broke ten-year-old.

Several days later, a couple of us "cowboys" decided we were going to ride the filly double even if it killed us. That proved to be impossible, she simply wasn't going to stand for it. She would go all day without a problem, you just could not put anyone on behind.

With the women's college being in Fulton and having an equestrian program, my buddies and I became acquainted with several of the young women that studied there. We had ample places to trail ride and the young women would come out when they could and ride, or just hang out with us. One afternoon, five or six of us were hanging out and decided to do some fun training in this big open area we had tilled up for an arena.

I saddled up the app filly for one of the girls and turned her loose to play. There were four of the women mounted, relaxing and playing in the makeshift arena. One of my buddies had taken a liking for Jackie, the lady on my horse, and he decided to run out and bail up behind her. Before I could utter any warning and him not knowing the horse's history, he had done a Lone Ranger right up on the backside of the cold backed appaloosa.

The filly exploded into a bucking fit. The first big hop she made, my buddy hit the dirt in a heap and the young lady's bottom became separated from the saddle by three feet. She came back to the saddle with such force it whiplashed her neck rendering her unconscious. The next big hop launched the seemingly lifeless, limp woman, high into the air. A mid-air pirouette and she was falling like an asteroid. She landed right on the top of her head. Jackie lay in the dirt, motionless, face down, in a semi-fetal position. Right away, I ran out to assess the extent of Jackie's injuries.

My buddy was moving around, half crying, trying to catch his breath and half laughing at what had happened. I wasn't laughing. Having witnessed the rodeo, I knew full well the girl hitting the ground as she had, might be injured seriously.

I had no medical training, but I knew not to move the unconscious victim. However, Jackie's friends were much closer than I and got to her first. Without considering the outcome, they rolled her over to see how bad she was hurt. Jackie's eyes were rolled back and her dirt covered face was pale and clammy. She was breathing, but very shallow.

Young and foolish, no one considered calling for help, me included. I managed to get a wet rag and placed it across her forehead in an effort to revive the fallen cowgirl. A few minutes had passed before she began to open her eyes and move around. Coughing, trying to catch her breath, she asked what had happened.

Jackie laid on the ground for a good half hour before she had enough sense about her to even get up. When she did get up, aided by my buddy and one of her friends, she decided she'd had enough riding for the day and asked her friends to take her home. The rest of us had had all the excitement we needed for one day as well.

Three days later I asked about Jackie's condition. She was okay but had no recollection of the days' events.

Eddie Baise

CHUTE DOGGIN

One late summer day, Robby and I loaded up our horses and headed to the Bison Aire. Henry had invited us down to help vaccinate calves. He had about fifty-five head to run through and was short on help.

We always jumped at the chance to go down and help. We never got paid any money, but we were able to work our horses and sometimes he would let us mess with the rodeo stock when we finished doing the tasks he had for us to do.

The calves were in a fifteen-acre pen, so all we had to do was just crowd them a little to get them in the barn where the head chute was. Most of the stock on the ranch ran wild and there was a half dozen of these calves that had no intention of going in the barn, much less getting put through a chute. We did, however, manage to get them in.

Each time a calf would run up to the chute, Henry would squeeze the catch gate down on its neck and it would begin bawling, bucking and fighting the entire time. Each one got a shot and an ear tag and the little bull calves we clamped. We spent close to two and a half hours getting all the calves run through and cleaning up what mess we had made.

Henry decided it was time to take a break, so we all sat around drinking water and talking about all the bumps and bruises we had accumulated during the last couple hours.

We hadn't been sitting long when Henry asked if we wanted to help get in a few dogging steers for the rodeo that was coming up in a few days. You could always bet Henry would have something else to do besides what he asked us to come down for.

We agreed to help, got to our horses and headed out to the pasture where the steers were. This stock got used in the rodeos just about once a month, so they weren't as wild as the calves we had worked earlier. We moved them to the arena with very little trouble. Henry wanted to cut out six or eight to see if they would be good enough for the cowboys, so we separated out the ones he pointed out, put them in a small pen behind the chute and let the rest out in a bigger pen further back behind the arena.

Henry looked at me and asked if I wanted to wrestle one of the steers. I explained I'd never dogged a steer before, but I was willing to learn. He said we were going to "chute dog" these steers because I hadn't done this before and he didn't want me getting hung up in a stirrup or getting hurt some other way.

Normal steer wrestling you would be mounted horseback. The steer would be in a chute right next to the "box" where you had your horse lined up ready to charge out when the steer was turned loose. "Chute dogging" however, was a little different.

Instead of being horseback, you stood near the front of the chute, placed your hands on the steers' horns and nodded your head for them to turn him out. The idea was to hang on as the steer charged out, get your heels dug into the dirt, stop the wild beast and flip him on his side. All this would happen in a matter of a few seconds. Henry explained all this and asked if I was ready to try one.

I had been listening closely to the details Henry laid out for me, so I gave him the okay and he ran the first steer in. He got me all lined up, hanging on to the horns and all, and asked if I was ready. I looked at him and he had a grin on his face that ran from ear to ear. I knew this was going to be exciting. I nodded ever so slightly and the chute opened with a bang.

I was sort of slight of build and when this four hundred-fifty-pound steer came out of the chute, it was all I could do to hang on. I managed to get my feet under me and get a good hold on the horns, as the steer is headed to the far end of the arena at a high rate of speed. I got my heels dug in and I hung on like a tick.

The only problem I was having was keeping my heels dug in. The steer had enough strength in his neck to lift me off the ground. The steer was running down the arena, I had a good grip on the horns and my heels were only hitting the ground every couple yards. I would plow the ground with my boot heels for a bit and then up I'd go, then back down and plow some more. I finally wore the little steer down in about forty yards and got him stopped. I was uncertain whether I flipped him, or he just toppled over from exhaustion, but he went over.

I got up off the ground and looked back at the chute to see everyone having a good laugh. I asked Henry if he thought I might make a steer wrestler and he was laughing too hard to answer. I did one more steer that evening and that was the extent of my steer wrestling career.

Eddie Baise

A LOST CALF

On a Saturday morning, I got a call from my neighbor, Carson, wanting to know if I could help round up some cows. I told him I'd be glad to help and asked if I should get a couple other riders to help. He thought that might be a good idea. I got on the phone and had a couple guys headed my way to help with the gathering. I saddled up this appaloosa I had just started about 30 days before. She was progressing fairly well and showed a little interest in cows, so I figured this little exercise would be good for her. It wasn't but a couple miles to the pasture where the cows were, so I put her in a short lope thinking this would take the "edge" off her and she would be settled by the time we got there. I arrived before any of the other riders, so while I waited I got the low down as to what was going on.

There were 30 cows with calves on a nearly treeless piece of ground measuring about a half mile square. The property laid pretty flat with a couple shallow draws running north to south about an eighth mile long. The wild brome had grown fairly tall and was in random patches.

The other riders had made it by now and Carson was ready to start bringing in the stock. The plan was to ride out, circle the herd and then slowly bring them into a makeshift corral. Then it would be possible to load the cattle in trailers for the move to a different pasture.

All the cows were near the back of the property quietly grazing on the late summer grass. I headed to the south and the other two riders went to the north. Everyone was going at a slow walk to avoid exciting the herd.

Things were going very well as the three of us got behind the now alert cows and curious calves. As we began to crowd the cows toward the corral, some of the calves would run and buck and others started pairing up with their mommas. While we moved the cows horseback, Carson stood inside the corral rattling a big can of corn attempting to motivate the cows closer to the open gate. Much to my amazement, my mount was moving the herd like she had done it a hundred times before. In about an hour or so we had the herd filing through the gate of the "V" shaped pen. While we moved the cow-calf pairs, Carson counted to ensure all were accounted for. With cows all in and the gate closed, we were informed one calf was missing.

I agreed to make a quick ride out to look for the calf, while the rest began to load the restless herd. The brome was tall enough for the little calf to hide in any of the grown-up patches. I elected to make a run down one of the draws that had very tall grass growing in it. My hunch paid off and about halfway down the draw, there laid the calf.

My horse hadn't seen the little black baby until it woke from its nap and jumped up in the middle of the grass patch just ahead of us. When the horse saw the calf jump up, she panicked and almost turned inside out trying to run away from whatever it was that had magically appeared before her. In her haste to escape, I ended up grabbing leather, hair, air or whatever I could to stay mounted. I managed to get my behind back on leather and my wide-eyed mount settled a couple hundred yards away. For a brief moment, calf and horse stood and eyeballed each other, waiting for one or the other to move. The calf made the first move upsetting the horse once again. This time, I was better set to react to the commotion and got control much quicker.

The calf had never seen a horse and it must have thought its world had come to an end. It took off across the pasture with its tail stuck straight up in the air. I figured I'd run up beside it and maybe turn it towards the bawling cows being loaded from the catch pen.

The calf ran nearly a quarter mile as hard as it could pace until it hit the line fence, my horse trying to keep pace. The scared calf hit the fence hard enough to break two fence posts, only slowing him briefly and then he was off again, back across the wide open pasture. I pulled my horse to a stop knowing I had no chance of ever getting the calf to the corral. I knew if I kept up the chase, it might run the calf to death.

I trotted back to the loading operation where the crew had been working and watching the spectacle unfold. Of course, I took a bunch of flack about letting one little black calf get the best of me.

After finishing loading the herd, the corral gate was opened back up and corn was put out. In two days the calf came in for a bite to eat, was caught and then united with its mother. As for that half app filly, every time she saw something black she'd get a little nervous and let out a loud snort.

Turned out, she wasn't a cow horse after all.

Eddie Baise

A FRIDAY NIGHT FIGHT

Dad and I had gotten into it again and this time it was so bad I was ready to hit him in the mouth with my fist. I had both hands tightly clenched ready to let him have one, then the other. He was equally angry and I was wondering who was going to throw that first punch. I took one step closer fully prepared to launch a barrage of flying knuckles and I saw the fear, or what I perceived as fear, in his eyes. Suddenly, something inside told me not to implement my attack. I turned and walked away, not saying one more word.

I had graduated high school that May, getting ready to turn eighteen that June, working a part-time day job, hauling hay at night or running and drinking all night if I wasn't hauling hay. Dad expected me to be at home when he got there so I could do "stuff" he needed to be done, when he wanted it done and how he wanted it done. If I wasn't, he would sometimes fly off the handle and go into a rage of ranting and raving like some wild beast. On more than one occasion he had threatened to shoot himself. This time, I offered to get his weapon of choice. I knew I shouldn't have said it, but I wasn't going to listen to more of his bellyaching or be his free labor anymore.

I stormed into the house, stomped upstairs and began to pack what clothes I could fit into a brown paper grocery bag. When I came back down the steps, my stepmother met me at the bottom.

"What are you doing? Are you okay?"

"I've had all his crap I can take, I'm leaving!"

"What happened?"

"We got into it, again. I can't take it anymore. I'll see you, Mom. Bye."

It hurt her that I was leaving, but I knew I couldn't stay. She knew it as well.

"Where are you going to stay?"

"Anywhere but here Mom." I turned and left.

I didn't see Dad when I backed out of the driveway and I didn't care where he had gone. All I knew, I had to get away from there and not look back.

I drove over to the stables where I had been keeping my horse even though the development project and the stables had been shut down for six months or better. No one was around, so I treated the place as if it was mine. There was no electric and I had to haul water for the horses, but it was fine for now and it wasn't costing anything but four dollars a month to haul the water I needed.

I sat in the truck thinking about everything that had happened minutes before and felt certain I had done the right thing in not hitting Dad. Had I proceeded with the altercation, it would have only served to divide us more, make things worse for my stepmother and it would have meant⋯ well, nothing good would have come out of it.

I milled around the stables for a while, thinking about where I might land for the night. I thought about going down to Robby's, but I really felt like I needed to be alone. I needed to sort through things and get my head cleared.

Finally, I thought about the little cabin that the development company used for a temporary sales office. It had plenty of space for me to stay in for a few nights if I needed to. The company hadn't collected any keys, or anything else for that matter when they pulled the plug and because I had been doing maintenance, I still had a key to every building on the project. I fired up the little blue Ford and drove a mile into the project.

As I pulled up to the cabin, the lights of the pickup reflected back into my eyes briefly hindering my vision. Hitting the dimmer button on the floorboard remedied the problem right away. I shut down the truck engine, sat for a few seconds to look things over, then proceeded to get out and walk up to the front porch with the key in my hand readied to unlock the front door.

We Were Cowboys

Opening the door I was presented with a musty smell from the little cabin being shut up for an extended period of time. All the electric throughout the project had been cut off due to delinquent bills, so I was feeling my way in the darkness hoping I'd not step on, or trip over any object, whether dead or living.

Managing to successfully maneuver towards a window, I cracked it just enough to let in a bit of fresh air. There was no furnishing left inside, so I was banished to the carpeted floor for the night.

The stress of the day before must have exhausted me because when I woke up, the sun was already shining brightly. Even though I was fully dressed, I was chilled from the cool air I had let in overnight. Slowly rising from the hard carpet covered floor, my body ached everywhere. Rubbing the caked on, crusty residue from the corner of my eyes, I sensed the room smelled a little better than the night before. I wanted coffee but had no means of making any, so I walked out onto the front porch and thought to myself, it's Saturday, you are free to do whatever you want. I decided to go to town and get breakfast!

The trip to town was only twenty minutes and I used the driving time to decide whether I was going to the Spot Café or Volleys. I surmised Volley's had two very attractive and friendly waitresses and felt that was the better choice of the two.

I sat down at a table, turned a cup over onto a saucer and waited for one of the ladies to greet me. As I had hoped, my favorite of the two came towards me and asked if I wanted coffee.

"Yes, Mam and two eggs, over medium, bacon and white toast, buttered."

Scratching on her pad and then poured a cup of aromatic heaven. Then she turned and walked straight away from me.

As she left to turn in my order, I watched her hips move from side to side under the short, tight uniform, reminding me of a fine quarter horse in motion.

She turned back around, catching me staring at her backside, smiled and asked, "Cream?"

I felt my face flush as I answered, "Yes, Please."

I was so embarrassed, I almost died right there.

Once the red had left my face, I thought about what had just taken place seconds before.

I couldn't imagine why I had made the comparisons that I had and I felt a couple things were for sure.

First, there was little doubt she had caught me looking at her hind-quarters. Secondly, had she known what I was thinking, she probably would not have taken my thought as complementary as I had thought it was.

We Were Cowboys

In just minutes, the smiling waitress returned with my meal, heated my nearly empty coffee cup and asked if I needed anything else. I couldn't answer. I just shook my head side to side indicating no. I quickly devoured my bacon and eggs as if I hadn't eaten in weeks, left a tip on the table, paid my tab and exited to my pickup just outside on 7th Street.

Returning to my little cabin on the lake, I looked around the interior to see just what was there. There was a short kitchen counter, probably only eight feet long, that had a double bowl stainless steel sink in it. There was a set of cabinets holding the top up and there were two narrow wall cabinets above. I raised the kitchen sink faucet handle up and of course, nothing exited the spout. I went on into the small living room and opened the sliding patio door all the way open to let in the spring breeze.

Going on into the bathroom, I discovered it was tiny. There was a shower, a stool and a very small lavatory, all situated to where I could have almost used all three at the same time. The last two rooms were bedrooms with a nice closet in each. I wondered where I could get a bed to sleep on if I stayed here long. I had done enough of the house tour and decided to go riding for a bit.

I spent most of the afternoon riding my horse. I didn't really go anywhere, I just rode the dirt roads the excavators had dozed out during the construction phase of the development. Altogether there were approximately thirteen miles of dirt paths, most without any gravel on them, which made a perfect place to ride a barefoot horse. It was nearing dusk by the time I decided to go back to the barn and put my ride up for the evening.

It was dark by the time I got back to the cabin and I thought about going out somewhere, it was Saturday night after all. Realizing I hadn't bathed for two days, I did a quick armpit check and postponed that idea completely. Mom and Dad would be going to church in the morning, I figured I'd go back home and get more of my stuff while they were gone. I went out to the truck, grabbed a pair of jeans from the paper bag serving as my suitcase and went back to the cabin. I rolled them into a tight roll, laid them under my head for a pillow and waited for sleep.

I timed my covert visit home perfectly. No one was there and the coffee was still warm in the percolator sitting on the countertop. I poured myself a cup, stirred in two heaping spoons of sugar and sat down to enjoy a cup of sweet, warm coffee before I collected more clothes.

I rinsed out the coffee mug and set it in the sink with the rest of the morning dishes, thinking nobody would notice. I climbed the wooden stairs up to what had been my room. I had shared the room with my brother and for all I cared, it was all his now. Filling another grocery sack, I turned to survey the room one last time to see if I had missed anything before descending into the kitchen once again. Catching a whiff of the awful odor I was emitting, I slipped into the bathroom and got my toothbrush, toothpaste and a new bar of soap.

I was in and out in less than fifteen minutes and no one would be the wiser. One last thought, get a blanket. I ran back in, grabbed the cover off my old bed upstairs and left in a cloud of dust.

There was a hole of water in the bend of the creek, which served as our party spot. It was just downstream from the remains of a bridge, which had been abandoned years ago after a big flood. There was a rope dangling from a big maple tree that was leaning at just the right angle to swing way out into the deep water. We'd build a fire and party half the night, drinking and swimming in the murky water.

I drove towards the swimming hole at Broken Bridge. I was going to get at least some of the stench off me. If that water was good enough to skinny dip in, it was good enough to take a bath in.

I drove the truck along the creek on the far side until I was almost able to step out of the cab and slide down the bank into the water. Peeling all my dirty clothes off, tossing them in the bed, I unwrapped the fragrant bar of soap and ran down into the cool spring water. Holding my breath, I dunked my head completely underwater and ran my fingers through my hair to get it soaked.

For the next few minutes, I rubbed the perfumed bar all over my soiled skin. It was such a good feeling. Dipping beneath the surface of the water once more, I rinsed off the bubbly suds allowing them to float down with the slow-moving current. Satisfied with my cleanliness, I emerged from the water causing goose bumps to rise over my entire body and streaked up the bank to the truck. I hadn't gotten any towels on my raid at home, so pulling my clothes on over my damp body without getting a sandy bonus was impossible. I'd have to deal with the sand later when I was dry. I pulled my boots on to my bare feet and fired the truck to get back to the privacy of the cabin.

 I got back to the cabin, shucked all my clothes while standing on the back deck and tried to shake the semi-dry sand loose. Beating the heel of my boot against the railing proved to be fairly successful in emptying the grit from there. Pulling my briefs off and using them as a cloth repelled the rest of the grime. Tossing the sandy underwear aside, I opted for another clean pair of shorts before redressing. I was supposed to help haul hay the next day, so I felt I would spend the rest of the day relaxing.

 As I sat on the front porch steps of the cabin, I ran the Friday night fight through once more. I knew I had done the right thing. However, I had a whole new set of problems to deal with, but I was on my own and I knew I'd figure out what to do.

We Were Cowboys

Best of all, I didn't have to answer to Dad any longer.

Eddie Baise

ROBBY LEAVES HOME

"Where have you been? I looked for you all weekend."

Robby and me, along with the last member of our hay crew, showed up at the fields to put up hay, but the owner had postponed the harvest due to chances of rain the next few days.

Robby began to question what I had done over the past weekend and I responded by filling him in on the details that had prompted my homesteading at the cabin. He went on about what I was going to do and where I was going to reside. I told him about staying at the cabin and since we didn't have to buck hay, I was going to the electric co-op to see about getting the power restored. If I got that accomplished, I would then get the place cleaned up and get water hauled into the cistern that was under the house.

The electric company was reluctant to reconnect the power to my residence, but I got with the right person, made the right statements and power was restored the next day. The process of making the place habitable, however, would take substantially longer and require a bit of backwoods engineering, something I was pretty handy at. Several pipes had ruptured from freezing and the water heater needed repairs as well, all things I managed to make operational. Once all the necessary repairs were completed, I wasn't forced to bathe in the swimming hole anymore.

I managed to come up with a bed with sheets and blankets, a small kitchen table that had been thrown away, a propane cook stove that I salvaged from the development company's cook shack and lastly, a small coffee pot to boil my morning beverage in. I figured I would gather additional furniture if I stayed in this location long.

About a week after I had gotten my new home livable, Robby asked if he could move in with me. Apparently, there was an incident between him and his dad that ended with similar results as mine. His mother felt in order to keep peace in the family, maybe the two of us could live together. I agreed. After all, we were best friends.

That same day, the other bedroom had a bed moved in and his mother brought all sorts of pots, pans, and dishes for us to use. She made and hung curtains, brought linens for the bathroom and even found an old used couch for the living room. She pretty much made a house into a home for the two of us in a matter of a couple days.

For the next eighteen months, Robby and I were together almost all the time. We rode horses, drank beer, worked down on the ranch on occasion, hauled hay, drank more beer, rode some more horses and lived a wild, immature and unintelligent lifestyle.

During this same eighteen-month period, I met a young woman from Fulton. We dated, I proposed and Jerri and I married a few months later.

Immediately after the wedding, I brought my bride to the homesteaded cabin to live and Robby moved out to live with his girlfriend at her place.

I can't say I settled down, I might have slowed down. Married life was much more different than I had envisioned and the wild and free habits of the past were difficult to quit.

ONE LAST RIDE

Rumors had it the owner had gotten into trouble and was going to prison. The ones doing all the talking didn't really know and the ones that did know weren't talking. All I knew was the Bison-Aire was closing down and would no longer be a working cattle ranch. I was losing the place I could go and do the things I wanted to do. The place I could go and be a cowboy, if only for a day.

I got wind of a family west of Fulton that had started a rodeo stock business. They were putting on bull buck-offs every so often to help with expenses to finance their endeavor. I kept thinking to myself I needed to check this outfit out to see how it was going. I had talked to a couple guys I knew and they had been to several of the rodeos. They told me I needed to come out as well. I knew however, I couldn't go and just watch, I would want to ride.

I had gotten married, we had a little boy and I had a full-time job working construction that kept me on the road a lot. It was difficult to get home early and when I did get home at a decent time, there was always some chore that needed attention. Finally, I decided I was going to the buck-off the coming Saturday.

I scrounged around all week looking for my gear and all I found was my old rusty spurs. It wouldn't matter though, someone would loan me whatever I needed.

With my wife and toddler in tow, I headed to the buck-off. It was a short drive across the county and in twenty minutes we parked in the lot behind the already full bleachers. I got the family seated and then I went to the cashier to get signed up for a ride. I quickly scoured over the cowboys in back of the chutes looking for someone I knew. Finally, I saw a few familiar faces and immediately began the process of procuring enough gear to make my ride. It wasn't long and I had the essentials, that most important bull rope, a good leather glove, a pair of chaps and my own spurs to top off the last of the equipment.

Several bulls were turned out and the crowd cheered as each rider made his eight-second attempt. I was up next. I could feel the blood pumping as I crawled over the chutes' sides and lowered my body down onto the restless, dirty bulls' back.

I handed the borrowed rope to the cowboy right next to me and he dropped one end beside the bulls' right side. Another cowboy grabbed the loose end and handed it back to me. Looping that end through the other, I placed the "handle" over the bulls' wither and pulled the whole rig tight onto my open hand that I'd placed in the handle.

"Tighter," I instructed and the cowboy pulled until I nodded. One wrap around my gloved hand imprisoned it within the tightly pulled rigging.

"You can't be a bull rider without a cowboy hat!" and someone, slapped an oversized western hat down on my head, covering my eyes.

My free hand pushed the big brimmed straw back, revealing my wife sitting in the bleachers, my son beside her, oblivious to what I was about to do. The Stetson rocking back and forth, I nodded I was ready and the gate swung open.

A substantial amount of time had passed since I had last bucked out anything, let alone a fifteen-hundred-pound bull. Almost immediately, I was pulled off the rope. I fought to regain my position squarely over the twisting, turning, bucking beasts' shoulders, but it proved futile and I was thrown to the tilled arena floor. I didn't waste any time regaining my feet, meanwhile looking for my unwilling host that had just tossed me aside. As I collected the borrowed gear, I was reminded by the announcer, "No time."

With a "Thanks.", I dispensed all the gifted equipment back to the rightful owners.

As I walked slowly back to join my family, I reflected on the evenings' ride. I was disappointed I hadn't covered my bull to make the eight-second buzzer. However, I thought, I did what I had come to do. I achieved the one thing I really needed, that unexplainable feeling, that indescribable rush, when I lowered my comparatively small and fragile body onto a massive rodeo bull that didn't want me there, and bet myself against the bull that I was going to come out on top whether I made a full eight-second ride or not.

Just as an addict, I knew it would be tough to never seek that "high" again, but I thought this should be, this would be my final bull ride.

THE BEGINNING OF THE END

About a year after Jerri and I married, Robby and his girlfriend married as well. As families we continued to socialize on a regular basis, but not to the extent we had before marriage. Robby and I had gone to work in construction, the same line of work, but different companies.

Robby and his wife had a son together, but they struggled and eventually divorced. His ex-wife took their son out of state and left Robby with financial troubles.

Robby wasn't the same person after that. It seemed to drive him down to a low I cannot describe. Eventually, he got hired on to the same company I worked for and we were together again, working for the same outfit. In time he would almost come back to the person I once knew.

After a while, Robby had a new girlfriend and they moved in together. Mary Anne rode horses as well and we would all get together often, having Saturday or Sunday trail rides with other families.

As our careers progressed, I became a foreman on the crew, Robby was lead man and we had one or two men that worked with us depending on the project size. We worked well together, everyone knew their job and we worked hard for several years without any problems. But as time went on, the pressures of the jobs, the constant push from the office to get the jobs done faster and being in the same proximity all the time, wore on mine and Robby's relationship.

I confronted Robby on an issue and we argued until he'd had enough of my bossing or I'd had enough of his rebellion. At any rate, neither of us was happy with the other and it put a wedge between us that pushed us far apart.

A year or so after the confrontation, I left the construction company I had worked at for fourteen years to take a similar position with a company starting up in Fulton. For me, it meant I would be much closer to home and I could spend more time with Jerri and our two sons. For Robby, it meant he was now in charge of the crew I'd left behind, a responsibility he did not want and he left the company only a few weeks after I did.

Robby and I continued to raise, ride and train horses. Our social life was almost non-existent, he made new friends and so did I. We were cordial when our paths crossed and we were

We Were Cowboys

still friends, but nothing like when we were younger.

My job took me on one avenue, Robby's on another. We didn't visit much anymore, we only lived a couple miles apart, but neither of us went out of our way to stay in contact with the other. Just in passing, I did see Robby on a fairly regular basis as I drove past his and Mary Anne's house trailer they called home.

I had noticed Robby appeared to be gaining weight. He had always been a good sized man, taller and heavier than me, but this was just getting fat I thought.

One afternoon, I saw him outside and I thought I'd stop to give my old friend some grief about his protruding stomach. I stopped in, got out of the truck and we greeted each other as we had a half million times before.

We chit-chatted for a bit and I interjected, "You're gonna have to quit drinking so much beer. You're getting fat!"

With a stone-cold face, he replied he'd not had a beer in three months, he hadn't felt like drinking and thought maybe something might be wrong. I told him he should seek medical advice and he responded he was in just a short while.

Robby did get medical attention and was diagnosed with a cancer. A tumor and a portion of his intestine were removed and after a stay in the hospital, he was sent home to recuperate.

One afternoon I stopped in to pay a visit to my convalescing buddy. He was understandably sore, somewhat depressed and looked under-weight now. He raised the gown he was wearing to show me the wounds left by the surgeon. I was shocked by the massive scar.

We spent a good hour or maybe longer, reminiscing about many of the things we had done as kids and adults. We talked about some of the horses we had ridden, the skinny dipping at the swimming hole, riding those first bulls at the Bison-Aire, the times that drove us apart and then, the things that would bring us back together again.

As I rose to leave, Robby extended his hand and I grasped it, holding on for a long moment. Even though we had been friends for what seemed to be forever, I could not recall ever shaking hands like that with Robby.

"I'll see you, friend," he said, slowly releasing his grip for me to leave.

I acknowledged his gesture and left wiping tears from my face.

About a week later, my friend of over thirty years succumbed to his illness.

Robby left a pregnant widow and a hole in me that could never be filled by another. I was saddened that he was gone and that I had not been a better friend, but I cherished the friendship we had and all the memories we had built together when we were kids, back in the days when we were cowboys.

   Later that same year, Mary Anne gave birth to a daughter.

To: Robin
From: Mama Cudd
Daddy Cudd
5-27-2018